Structopathic children

I

D1374031

Modern approaches to the diagnosis and instruction of multi-handicapped children

9

Structopathic children

A sociotherapeutic treatment type

Part I
Description of disturbance type and strategies

J. F. W. Kok

Professor of special psychology and special education, University of Utrecht

1972

Rotterdam University Press

Translated from the original Dutch publication 'Struktopathische kinderen, een orthopedagogisch behandelingstype' (L.C.G. Malmberg, 's-Hertogenbosch) by A. de Bruyn, E. van den Ing and Mrs. W. L. van Os.

ISBN 90 237 4109 9
Printed in the Netherlands

Contents

Acknowledgments

We should like to record our grateful thanks to the young patients and staff of the residential treatment centers of Roelant, Berk en Beuk and St. Michiel, all three situated near Nijmegen, in the Netherlands, whose co-operation enabled us to accomplish this study, both clinically and experimentally. One thanks goes in particular to Mr. and Mrs. Obbens who made the 'impossible possible'.

Dr. O. R. Hommes, neurologist, drs. R. L. 't Lam and drs. Th. H. J. Gijsbers, psychologists, provided from their disciplines the data concerning the experimentally treated children. We are also deeply indebted to them for their elaboration on the treatment type.

During the period preceding clinical research, our work also benefited from the diagnostic data provided by dr. A. P. J. Meyknecht, psychiatrist, and drs. Th. Verhoeven, psychologist.

It was possible to treat a larger number of therapy groups thanks to the help of the group therapists, Mrs. Th. Klomp and Mrs. R. Ockhuyzen.

We are also most grateful to the translators, Mr. A. de Bruyn, Mr. E. van den Ing and Mrs. W. van Os, who spared no pains in entering into the terminology of the subject.

Finally, I should like to acknowledge the invaluable assistance of Mrs. T. Cremers, who patiently and stoically typed and re-typed the manuscript.

Introduction

This study has several characteristics which make it rather difficult to fit in with other studies. More important than the fact that it is a mere contribution to the treatment of a type of disturbed children, is the way in which it was carried out. A more original and realistic approach is bound to be more rewarding and a multi-disciplinary procedure can and should be applied to other types of deviations as well. This book tries therefore to suggest ways of getting us out of the impasse.

Total, full-time treatment, supported by planning and organization, is not all we aim at. For this is no more than a half-truth. The necessity of taking the type of patient system into account is easily overlooked. Procedure and treatment will suffer from 'methodologitis': dangerous generalizations will develop, resulting in a formal and meaningless system.

Total treatment also presupposes that we start from the complete individual, in his relation to his full-life situation. This entails more than just coupling aspects of treatment to diagnostic data. If normal development does not get going or is hindered, we, as social individuals, are confronted by a human being, imposing a 'demand' on us. A demand to create situations which will offer him chances of growth. Individual diagnostics and situation analysis (for children related to their up-bringing) analyse this 'demand', but do not define it at first. An integrated, multi-disciplinary approach analyses the 'demand' in such a way that a complete and realistic picture evolves. In so far as disturbed individuals can be included in this type of 'demand', they constitute a *disturbance type*. The 'answer' is a *first grade strategy*. It is sociotherapeutic (Edelson) in the full sense of the word. In our opinion, the sociotherapist does not only contribute considerably to analysing the 'demand', he also directs the treatment in all its aspects. If 'demand' and 'answer', disturbance type and first grade strategy, are well geared, we refer to a *sociotherapeutic treatment type*.

Secondly, these principles resulted in the description of a first treatment type: structopathic children. Let us elucidate: structopathic children correspond to a certain extent to hyperkinetic children. They suffer from choreatiform hyperactivity, among other things, but their disturbance is more serious, so personality disturbance becomes a problem to the parents even during infancy. The sociotherapeutic approach, requiring an integrated multi-disciplinary procedure to describe the disturbance type, leads to a new point of view. This is not only essential for 'diagnostics', but is a realistic, operational starting-point for overall treatment. The simplistic link: medical defect – partial treatment of it (fight against symptoms) is avoided. Our 'answer' is to create a world offering optimal chances of growth. This is quite different from stimulus reduction.

A third important item is the experimental approach, besides the clinical method. An essential second grade strategy is structuring group therapy. This has not been subjected to clinical tests alone. Method and results were also experimentally tested in Nijmegen. This has not been very common procedure, especially in child psychotherapy. Admittedly, some examinations only test one detail among some children. But thorough examination of the total treatment situation is something quite different. Results of this examination and their discussion took up so much space that we have had to publish them separately (volume II).

I hope this study will have contributed towards the treatment of a type of disturbed children, but especially have stimulated these methods of examination and treatment of other types.

1. Sociotherapeutic classification of treatment types and preliminary differentiation

1. SOCIOTHERAPEUTIC APPROACH AS AN ALTERNATIVE

Anyone occupied in treating disturbed children is confronted with various theories. At the same time he is faced with the fact that many patients show no results. In other words: the applicability of the treatment theories is limited, or perhaps specific.

Dissatisfaction has been increasing during the last few decades. This has a number of consequences. Some people are becoming pessimistic: is it in fact possible for serious cases to be treated successfully? (Robins). Others are aiming at a change from part-time therapies to round-the-clock-treatment (Redl-Wineman).

Apparently a different approach to the problems is required to lead us out of the impasse. It is not merely a matter of the degree of change, but rather of the need for structural change. Investigation of three factors will lead us to an alternative approach.

Diagnosis and treatment

Of the two, diagnostics has clearly developed most. The pediatrician and neurologist on the one hand and the psychologist on the other can tell us much about child deviations. Two types of problem however arise.

Considering diagnostics first, neurodiagnostics and psychodiagnostics should ideally work together closely and try to determine the individual child's deficiencies. They should then aim at ascertaining how the child's failure is bound up with the established defects. This faces us with a new problem: quite often it is not only hard to link up the deviations, but it is often more difficult to determine whether every deviation causes deviating behavior. To what extent should we emphasise each individual deviation in the pattern? The more indications of more absolute or more relative (age-inadequate) deviating behavior we find, the greater the variations in

1

patterns and ever-changing gradations will become. The additional factor of milieu does not simplify the problems (and if it is relevant, how?).

A second remark is more essential to our argument. Diagnostics provides guidelines for treatment, a situation which would indeed seem fairly ideal. However, in most cases no more than rather vague advice will be the result. By this stage parents should know that they must be tactful and patient and show a great deal of affection. Even so, science says nothing if many cases do not show results or if the situation deteriorates. To top it all, science blockades itself with the crushing argument that the parents set about it wrongly. Even a fairly ideal situation does not solve matters. Suppose a child has been examined neurologically and psychologically; it is a very clear case and it is generally agreed that he is of disturbance type X. Suppose another child is clearly of this type too. Obviously similar treatment will as a rule be advised for both children, for example in the same group of a residential treatment center. In sociotherapeutic practice children with a similar diagnosis do not only prove to behave differently outside the situation in which they are examined, but also react differently to similar treatment and need of differently-focused treatment. We can make this theoretical example more concrete with the case of two girls from one of the experimental groups, who were treated within the scope of this study. This is a case of monozygotic epileptic twins with an identical neurological and an almost identical psychological diagnosis. It was obvious that both in the real life situation and in the school situation of the residential treatment center and of group psychotherapy, both children had to be approached differently. Initially identical treatment proved to be successful with one girl, whereas the condition of the other one deteriorated.

This example is only one of many. In view of many years of experience we maintain that directions for treatment cannot simply be inferred from diagnostics. We shall also need data of the child's real life situation. We shall return to that later. These data do not replace diagnostics. Diagnostics continues to be necessary, but should be complemented, clarified and modified according to observation data, with, if drawn from real life, constitute new and co-structuring evidence.

Treatment and indoctrination

Little scientific attention has been paid to the treatment of disturbed children up to now. Psychotherapeutic theories designed for adults, which were copied slavishly far too often, gave rise to absolute points of view and generalizations.

Somebody finds himself confronted with people with specific difficulties. Great concern and many years of steady labor result in a treatment method. Although the method was originally evolved for a specific disturbance type, this is soon forgotten. The tendency to generalize comes into force. This phenomenon is often corroborated in the following way. The new method involves a particular view of Man, who is considered to be noble and high-principled. Making this absolute is but a step: this view should be the basis of human activity and treatment.

Partial theory, mostly not even evaluated yet, deteriorates into indoctrination. All its symptoms become apparent: inflexibility, intolerance, aggressiveness. Dissentients are attacked and reviled. We are concerned that this narrowing of mind leads to the foolish notion that all disturbance types can be helped by this method. The many types of disturbed children can only be helped effectively if individuality theories are abandoned. The disturbed child itself should be the center of all treatment. Unbiased and accurate observation may lead to a thorough and scientific knowledge of both child and treatment. Every treatment type requires its own methods, which cannot be applied outside the treatment for which they were developed.

Up-bringing and sociotherapy

Disappointing results with part-time therapies set people thinking about full-time treatment. Attempts are being made to transfer the situation in individual or group psychotherapy to the real life situation. However ingenious or progressive this may seem, it is still unusual. Real life is adjusted to the artificial situation. The danger of indoctrination is again great. Some advocates of psychiatric treatment think it advisable to replace up-bringing and education with analysis (Klein).

In the field of physical hygiene the case is as follows: Public health benefits from the results of medical science in this respect. Disease control provides information to keep the population healthy. But nobody is foolish enough to admit all healthy people into hospital. Nor is there any attempt to transfer hospital rules, habits and procedures to our homes, workshops, schools, camping sites, movie theaters, etc. The same applies to the treatment of problem children. We shall have to start from the real life situation. If there is something artificial about it to start with, e.g. treatment in a residential center, the community should be as normal as possible. That is to say, imitation of therapy hours is out of the question. These situations and the concomitant cure should be handled with extreme care. Psychotherapy might be helpful.

All people who function reasonably in bigger and smaller communities

3

are brought up in families. By this we mean that relationships with parents, brothers and sisters affect development, not education from scholastic teaching and training. Family influence can be minimized. Abuses do indeed occur. A question of paramount significance is to what extent much failure is occasioned by science. Inadequate criticism, especially of psychotherapeutic theories, has caused a great deal of uncertainty and rationalization among parents. They must feel sure, be at ease, spontaneous and confident of giving a successful up-bringing. The majority of adults react well, thanks to the family situation in their own childhood.

Good up-bringing stimulates development and growth, as well as having an educative influence on children. A minor part of this is effected by directed planning: the intentional aspect. For a greater part however real-life situations, and especially their climate, contribute towards up-bringing: the functional aspect. Children are sensitive to atmosphere and to being completely belonging, which is a stimulus for successful participation. A climate of basically healthy situations makes for a *constant and healthy* development. This is what the treatment situation is like. Situations in round-the-clock treatment must always be handled in such a way as to supply optimal and constant chances of recovery and growth. A therapeutic climate makes for a *recovering* development. A therapeutic, 'total treatment' situation, which is very close to real life and normal up-bringing, is called the *sociotherapeutic situation*. Sociotherapy must try to create such situations.

2. SOCIOTHERAPEUTIC TREATMENT TYPES

The concept of a sociotherapeutic treatment type brings us nearer to a solution. We shall first define it briefly, then clarify it with examples of structopathic children, as the first sociotherapeutic treatment type.

Agology versus diagnostics, a mistake

Several types of methodical assistance have been developed. Their study is called agology, the doctrine of acting methodically. Social technology is another term in use.

A particular aspect of this development is essential to our subject. There is a strong tendency to direct all treatment solely from agology. From an enormous body of methods and techniques one or more are drawn, to initiate a treatment. One-sidedness is a primary danger. Before long a method is considered generally applicable, although it was, as a rule, only developed in a limited field. Again we find a dangerous tendency to generalize. In a way this is bound up with methodology and technology being taken as philosophy.

A second item is no less dangerous. There are some over-ardent supporters of this new field of science who no longer feel inclined to take account of the diagnostic data of physicians and psychologists. In their opinion, action and treatment should be exclusively within the scope of agology. Others are of the opinion that diagnostic data are not to be ignored, though their agogic applicability is still open to discussion.

However a one-sided approach to the new line of agology will lead us nowhere. Instead of fusion, tension is the result. In our opinion the problem needs to be approached differently.

Disturbance type

The concept 'sociotherapeutic treatment type' is made up of two components; 'disturbance type' and 'first-grade strategy'.

By 'disturbance type' we mean specific behavior problems, manifested in mainly identical features by children or adolescents, which can be taken as representing a uniform requirement of identical therapeutic treatment.

It is therefore essential that disturbed behavior be diagnosed. If this disturbance leads to specific psychological and/or biological characteristics, children who do possess the diagnostic characteristics, partially or completely, but do not exhibit the specific behavior, should not be included in this type of disturbance. In this respect Slavson would seem to be nearer to the truth than Cruickshank. For Slavson points out that a child with minimal brain damage will not necessarily manifest poorly-structured behavior, but could become neurotic as well. (Slavson, 1952).

Cruickshank, on the other hand, generalizes when rejecting non-directive play-therapy for *all* brain-damaged children (Cruickshank, p. 238).

The disturbance type is not only determined from an agologic scientific point of view, but agology does play a part. The development and maturation of a type of disturbance is the tangent plane of behavior science, biology and agology. The first two provide a diagnosis in a strict sense, the last provides the necessary contribution concerning behavior analysis in the real-life situation. This includes the possibility of having a sociotherapeutic relationship (as well). The disturbance type is not the sum of different disciplinary data. The aim is not only to assess the significance and value of one contribution on another, but to proceed to a joint effort to

5

scrutinize the data in such a way that these elucidate, complement and explain one another. This is surely genuine intercorrelation. A discussion on structopathy could provide a concrete demonstration.

Strategies

In this way we get a picture, applying to both theoretical science and to the clinical treatment of individual cases. This will be our point of departure, as far as treatment is concerned. The sociotherapist now initiates a schedule of treatment, not focused on the individual, but as a general answer to the type of disturbance. He is not concerned with the individual's general background, but he creates a complex and coherent entity, the individual aspects of which may need new amplification. He takes diagnostics into account, because he starts from the jointly developed point of departure, the disturbance type. This supplies connecting and starting points for treatment. The treatment program, a general answer to the disturbance type, and applying to all individuals who can be included in this type, is called *first-grade strategy*.

This type of general treatment schedule, the first-grade strategy, is not an abstraction, but a concrete and programmed entity, which can really be applied. The term, 'general' does not imply a departure from reality, but refers to the fact that broad outlines are given. These outlines need particularizing, both as to aspects of treatment and as to individual nature.

In the first case we speak of *second-grade strategies*. For within the first strategy, drawn up for instance in a residential setting and put into effect in the real life situation (in a cottage), assistance is aimed at. It may consist of various types of function-training, social group work, psychotherapies and special education, just to mention a few. The first-grade strategy tells which second-grade strategies are needed, their value, their application and their general coherence. This is genuine intercorrelation.

Third-grade strategies are individual variations within the first and second-grade strategies. The structopathic child suffering in addition from slight vital formalism on the basis of vegetative lability, or his counterpart beginning to realize the missing father figure, needs individual adjustment of the general planning. But in this case too variations within the first-grade strategy are involved.

If the first-grade strategy provides an adequate answer to the disturbance type as a point of departure to treatment, then both components constitute

6

a sociotherapeutic treatment type. In the foregoing we hope to have indicated sufficiently that team research, while studying, observing and experimenting, is essential for the development of sociotherapy.

Treatment type and admission

But there is more to it. The definition of sociotherapeutic treatment type can be the goal and criterion of admission to a sociotherapeutic residential treatment center. This enables the center in its entirety, in its organisation and communication, in its equipment and in the training of its assistants, to be imbued with a first-grade strategy. At the same time an adequate therapeutic climate can be achieved. Real education and treatment is possible within the cottage, because individual variations tend to be within the scope of uniform, total planning. There must be no mistake about this. We do not for instance intend to place in a cottage a whole group of anxious or aggressive children. Symptom-based identity is not involved, but similarity in disturbance type is. A syndrome, if you like, considering that the point of departure is duly included in a particular approach, resulting from the disturbed behavior. Within a sociotherapeutic treatment type, sub-types can be differentiated. Sthenic and asthenic types, inhibited and acting-out questionary types are found among children requiring a disengaging approach. We have already mentioned free variation within the cottage. This remains, but the basic approach and broad outlines of treatment are the same; not because one view is generalized or one hobby applied, but because the patients, i.e. disturbance types require it. In other words, it will be possible to educate and treat within a cottage, using the approach of the group as a group, and group processes.

Neither admission nor staff evaluation of case discussions end in purely individual treatment planning: the treatment program as first and second-grade strategies has already been embodied in the organisation as change agent. Individual variations are the only ones to be considered and tested.

3. PRELIMINARY DIFFERENTIATION

The group of children and adolescents which, for convenience, is called the 'behavior disorders' group (maladjusted children or children with conduct disorders) as distinct from sensorially deficient, oligophrenic and physically handicapped children, is very heterogeneous. Often parents and group-workers are good at assessing the difficulty of such children and at characterizing them by comparison: 'Albert is just like our Eric', or: 'This new kid strongly reminds me of Spiro who used to be in cottage 3'.

Of course we run the risk of using the term 'difficult' in the sense of 'giving trouble', which would be odd. In this way some autistiform children would not manifest behavior disorders.

'Difficult' relates to the possibility of establishing a therapeutic relationship. Establishing a relationship and assessing its extent is a matter of experience and feeling. The extent to which this feeling proves to have been correct cannot be established until later, sometimes not until the education period is finished. In that sense the concept cannot be effectively employed. Besides, it does not infer direct treatment.

Psychotherapeutic experience

Sociotherapeutic treatment primarily demands a specific form of treatment. This fresh approach will shed light on the problem now that part-time play-therapies are being set up. What questions do these answer? By what criteria can they be assessed?

In practical therapeutic work, as done in the residential treatment center, some children are excluded from psychotherapeutic treatment. Their behavior grows more chaotic, their personality deteriorates and therapeutically speaking, the possibility of communication decreases. This is sometimes expressed by saying: 'We have lost our hold on them'.

There should be no mistake about this. Criteria for admission clearly determine whether this is actually experienced in every treatment center. If the children have been selected on their non-directive psycho-therapeutic communication for example, and if the selection has been performed well, the claim does not apply, though this does not detract from the matter at hand. A given therapy might then be assumed to have some application for all types of children with behavior disorders. In that case results will have to prove whether this line of thought can be maintained. Exclusion in practice, as indicated above, is to a large extent bound up with a lack of results. One must also take into account that this selection by exclusion on the basis of therapeutic experience should not be confused with what Corsini states. For he has variations in mind, based on the individual characteristics of the therapist, within an adult disorder group, which is essentially susceptible to one or more already existing psychotherapies. (Corsini, 1957, p. 55).

A selection of various forms of psychotherapy is also found in literature, either explicitly or implicitly.

In contrast with Melanie Klein's views Anna Freud limits child analysis to children having infantile neuroses. 'Dagegen hat sich in einer Diskussion dieser Frage ergeben, dass die meisten Wiener Analytiker einen andern Standpunkt vertreten und meinen, dass die Analyse eines Kindes nur im Falle einer wirklichen infantilen Neurose am Platze ist' (A. Freud, p. 9). The discussion of some cases confirms this and raises the question whether infantile neuroses only occur and can be treated among very intelligent children.

Other child-analytists have subsequently pointed out the necessity of being neurotic, of having complexes, in order to be entitled to treatment. Rambert speaks of 'extériorisation du conflit' (p. 18) and the treatment being directed at 'les complexes profonds' (p. 30). 'Il ne s'agissait plus désormais', Smirnoff states, 'de compenser un défaut intellectuel ou instrumental, ni de corriger les conditions extérieures défavorables, mais de dépister la cause étiologique de telle ou telle conduite, envisagée en tant que symptomatique d'une structure névrotique ou d'un trouble réactionnel' (p. 26). He expects in the child the healthy possibility that he can participate and assert himself in clearing internal psychical conflicts, which can then be regarded as structure-favoring: ' à permettre à l'enfant de modifier la structure sousjacente de sa personnalité et de rendre possible, par la solution des conflits intrapsychiques, de trouver un mode adaptatif plus satisfaisant' (p. 27).

A cognate line of thought is found in Sandschulte' s writings. She speaks of 'Zurückhaltung' and has the child take the lead (p. 84). Her quoting of Slavson (1956, p. 15) that the goal of child therapy is 'die Fähigkeit zu stärken, mit anderen Menschen mitzufühlen, d.h. positive Identifikationen aufzubauen' (p. 85) is another indication that she has a specific type of children in mind.

Zulliger who more clearly employs therapeutic play as such, and not as a means of interpretation – 'man kann ein Kind durchaus dauerhaft heilen, ohne dass ein einziges Wort der Deutung im orthodoxen, analytischen Sinn gebraucht wird' (1957, p. 44) – and consequently may offer assistance to a greater range of disturbed children, nevertheless presupposes conflicts.

'Bei jüngeren Kindern haben die Spiele den Zweck: 1. den pathogenen Konflikt in ihnen aufzudecken; 2. ihn psychotherapeutisch zu bearbeiten, der Konflikt wird dramatisch, agierend abgewandelt und gelöst' (1952, p. 86). In another book he speaks of 'eine Triebäuszerung (die) sich fixiert hat' and which is solved by play therapy, after which 'die Weiterentwicklung freie Bahn hat' (1953, p. 111). One question which comes to mind is what to expect when a neurotic superstructure, with a regulating and formalising function as a protective mechanism against a chaotic substructure, is dismantled.

Städeli states that he applies play therapy to more types of deviant children than is feasible with A. Freud's child analysis. He would seem to be proffering a tentative differentiation in treatment types. In the first place there are a number of types of children with behavior disorders, including children with minimal brain damage, who are considered to constitute one group for treatment: neurotic children with 'neurotischen Reaktionen' and 'einfachen Reaktionen' on the basis of 'mütterlicher Frustrationen' (p. 251). That is why Städeli presupposes a sound, spontaneous inner growth capacity, evident in his view that, from the first phase of therapy the child pushes through to the second, the more creative one, 'ohne irgendwelche Beeinflussung durch den Therapeuten' (p. 253).

Another typical feature of this group is that they can be overwhelmed by passion, which is a disturbing experience for the child and is followed up by embarrassment. For this reason, it would seem to us, these neurotic children differ from children, whose life is passion and who can be shattered by eruptive rage, but who afterwards have no recollection or reflection regarding it.

Beside this group of neurotics Städeli has a second treatment type. He mentions the necessity of specific manipulation for 'affektiv und erzieherisch verwahrlosten, chronisch deprimierten, in der affektiven Entwicklung verhinderten, ichschwachen und agierenden Kindern' (p. 253), involving the handling of materials before there is the opportunity of engaging in play. The goal of this 'material-therapy' is not indicated, so that this separate group is hardly characterized as a treatment type. Clearly, this other possibility was not further developed, because one model, with adapted strategy, was dealt with.

Annemarie Dührssen, whose work can be included in the psychoanalytic field even though she applies a rather eclectic method, is not explicit whether she limits herself to specific types of deviant children in her therapeutic activities.

However, it appears from her general views (p. 13), her description of child analysis (p. 238), discussions of psychoanalytic help with learning difficulties (p. 308f) and – especially – from casuistry, that she works with 'neurotics', adults, adolescents and children, whose development progress has come to a standstill midway, due to disturbing effects of the milieu.

Provisional conclusions

The discussion of some distinguished child psychotherapists, who base their procedures on psychoanalytic theory and its models, affords some items important for this argument. First of all the therapist either expressly states that psychotherapeutic treatment can only help certain groups of children whose up-bringing has become a problem, or this can be read between the lines, notably in casuistry. If contact with children who are not primarily neurotic is frequent, it is not clear whether these children are not after all on a par with primary neurotics owing to handling the same models as regards treatment type.

As a result of his view on maturation and development Spitz (1959) states: 'the essence of psychoanalytic treatment is that it does not direct, advise, educate. It liberates the personality and permits it to make its own adjustments' (p. 100). Psychical development, however, is described by him as follows: 'It covers the modifications imposed on the congenital equipment (both on maturation and on the other intrinsic factors of biological development) partly by environmental circumstances, partly by stress or by facilitation occurring among the factors operating in maturation and biological development' (p. 12). A second point is then raised: if psychical development is primarily disturbed because of disturbances in or a disturbed functioning of the constitution, of maturation or of biological development, will then in all cases a liberating and permissive approach be sufficient? In the majority of cases this takes place no more than one or a few hours a week. Congenital disturbances, that manifest themselves as oligophrenia, need no discussion. Children whose average mental performance is moderate to good, present a more difficult case. A limitation of the theory, that presupposes in all an adequate spontaneous inner growth capacity, or inadequate discrimination between theory and model, may lead to generalization of treatment.

Non-directive play therapy

The presupposition that every individual has the growth capacity to enable him by means of a liberating approach to take the first steps himself with initial or repeated self realization, is of essential moment in Rogers's theory.

As early as 1939, before his publications on non-directive psychotherapy, he wrote 'If the child is to gain real help to grow in his own way toward goals of his own choice, the therapist must create a relationship where such growth can take place .... There must be a willingness to accept the child

11

as he is, on his own level of adjustment, and to give him some freedom to work out his own solutions to his problems .... In psychotherapy the aim is to leave the major responsibilities in the hands of the child as an individual growing toward independence' (p. 282–283). Later on this is sharply defined: 'The individual has within himself the capacity and tendency, latent if not evident to move forward toward maturity' (1961, p. 35).

In this process of growth the non-directive relationship as such has full emphasis (1942, p. 30). To be able to realise this relationship the therapist should meet three fundamental characteristics, viz. 'therapist congruence, unconditional positive regard' and 'accurate empathic understanding' (1957; also see 1967, p. 98–106).

It is exactly when these characteristics involve entering a relationship and can only find their realization therein, that the patient's possibilities and modes of response are involved in this process.

Finally Rogers presupposes that ego and self already function: where the relationship between self structure and experience is diminished, psychotherapy can achieve that 'the structure of self now being much more congruent with the sensory and visceral experience of the individual' (1951, p. 530).

Closely related to Rogers is Allen (1942), who has the following theme in his study of psychotherapy: 'Children with personality and behavior difficulties can be helped to help themselves'.

The case studies in chapters 5, 6 and 7 leave no doubt about the application of this principle.

Axline (1947) subscribes almost literally to Allen's view. The second chapter of her book is entitled 'A method of helping problem children help themselves', to be elaborated in: 'Play therapy may be directive in form or it may be non-directive: the therapist may leave responsibility and direction to the child. It is with the latter type of play therapy that we shall be concerned' (p. 9). Her eight fundamental rules for non-directive play therapy (p. 75–138) are consistently synthesized from this point of departure.

Tausch advances the Rogerian theory and its model in Germany. He ascertains empirically that the Rogerian basic attitude is eminently suited for democratization of instruction and education (1967). In his 1956 publication, where he first expounds play therapy, he adopts Axline's fundamental rules. Tausch excludes children as well. 'Ausgenommen von dieser Therapie sind Kinder, deren Unangepasztheit auf einer krankhaften organischen Grundlage beruht .... Diese Erscheinungen sind nicht auf Grund von Lernvorgängen erwachsen, und Änderung dieser organischen

Störungen durch Lernvorgänge wird im allgemeinen sehr gering sein'
(p. 25). 'Von Psychotherapie ist ferner zu trennen die Heil- und Sonder-
pädagogik. Hier handelt es sich im allgemeinen um andauernde erziehe-
rische Bemühungen an Kindern mit offensichtlich strukturbedingten
organischen Defekten' (p. 12). The first exclusion seems particularly
strange to us, as if diffuse organic pathology invariably resulted in behavior
disorders. And if so, as if they are such that neurotisation and adequate
non-directive treatment have contrary indications by definition. The
criterion 'resulting from learning processes or not' also seems open to
question, because the problems of the organically handicapped child have
also been, perhaps for a major part, caused by learning processes. The
question remains whether this manner of classification, incorrect in our
view, is not founded on treatment typification, based solely on medical
diagnostics.

Group psychotherapy

Two important therapists have not been mentioned so far. Because they
primarily occupy themselves with group therapy, their classification into
treatment types is not so much concerned with the criterion: being suited
or not for liberating, disengaging treatment, but with the differentiation
principle: group therapy or individual therapy. (In this connection also
see Bach, pp. 12–18, and Corsini, 1957, p. 49 f).

Ginott (1961) defends group therapy (p. 1–28). It is not entirely clear to
what extent he makes a distinction in possibilities of treatment between
children with severe behavior disorders and neurotics. But he does say:
'The aggressive behavior may occur at home, at school, in the neighborhood, or in all these places. When the child misbehaves only at home but
not outside of it (or vice versa), it may indicate that the core problem is a
reactive and unconsciously retaliatory way of life against real or fancied
mistreatment by parents. In such a case, group therapy is the treatment of
choice' (p. 23). This indication for group therapy implicitly contains an
additional distinction as to the degree of behavior disorders. One might
occasionally wonder whether there are among the types of deviating
children he discusses (p. 37–50) some who are on the verge of being
neurotic and having severe behavior disorders. In this respect Ginott does
not give his opinion upon the manner of treatment. From his observations
he appears to specialize in the treatment of intelligent, slightly neurotic
children.

In his discussion of the basic aims of psychotherapy, Slavson is in favor
of different ways of treatment for different disturbance types. He limits

treatment by this psychotherapy to neurotic children. 'In larger terms, the major aim of psychotherapy is to eliminate self-encapsulation by eliminating or reducing self-protective or retaliatory rigidities established in childhood and to weaken the defenses built up as a reaction to earlier stresses and traumata' (1952, p. 142). Elsewhere he mentions again his distinction between those who can and those who cannot be treated: 'We are prepared to say with some degree of certainty that clients with unmistakable psychoses or psychopathy and severe behavior disorders do not respond to free group pressure and are therefore a poor treatment risk in group therapy' (1960, p. 83). Now Slavson's problem of making a selection for group treatment, which we mentioned before, becomes apparent, and we may not conclude that he indicates suitability for treatment without comment. Anticipating a more specific point of view we can also note that on the one hand he does not state that someone unsuited for group therapy can invariably be helped by individual psychotherapeutic treatment, especially if mere encapsulation is involved. On the other hand it is debatable whether other assistance should be individual.

When children suited to his treatment are 'neurotic' Slavson uses the term 'social hunger' (1960, p. 85) or 'his desire to be accepted, to be with a group and a part of it' (ibid., pp. 84–85). He mentions four criteria from an unpublished study by Gertrude Goller, which are indicative that this situation exists and consequently that group treatment is possible.

The question arises of how to assess and treat children whose social development stagnates or does not get going at all and who are not desirous of contact in this way. The same question also crops up when over-aggressive behavior is taken as a reaction to fears resulting from being abnormally frustrated, for a longer period or very intensely. 'The over-aggressive child finds relief from his anxiety in such a group, while the shy and withdrawn overcomes his fears.' (ibid. p. 84). In this case a distinction is made between more sthenic and more asthenic neurotic types, possibly slightly more formalistic. No attention is paid to aggression as a symptom of being differently disturbed; to aggressive or acting-out behavior which is not reactive and which is certainly not experienced as such (not even subsequently), but which is no more than a symptom of disintegration or a partial, non-integrated break-through of passion.

Finally Slavson clearly favors a classification of treatment types on the basis of the nature of disturbed behavior: '.... in choosing clientele for therapy groups, the symptom picture is initially relied upon and not clinical or diagnostic categories' (ibid. p. 83). The application of this criterion is evident from the fact that a medical criterion such as organicity is not decisive for classification in treatment types as is demonstrated by:

14

'The treatment of a neurotic nine-year-old boy with organic deficiency' (1952, ch. XI). It is not our concern whether a client is organically defect, but in what way the personality has developed in the milieu on the basis of this deficiency, or, in some cases, in spite of the deficiency; whether a 'disengaging' approach is possible and if not, what manner of treatment would be productive, in view of behavior in (sociotherapeutic) circumstances.

Conclusions

It is probably worth presenting once again the reasons for one discussing some of the leading child psychotherapists. It was not our intention to view these procedures in a negative and critical way. On the contrary, these therapies can help a considerable number of children whose up-bringing and self realization were in danger. Help by means of psychotherapeutic methods can be such that they are freed from causes that hinder their development, and will once more stand a chance of healthy development and growth. Viewed from another standpoint: that the real life situation, in which they may grow and develop, and which is therefore educative, is restructured so as to facilitate up-bringing and self realization again. For lack of better terminology, these children are labeled neurotic in this study. They need acceptance and a liberating approach. This will be dealt with in more detail in chapter 2.

We have sought in our survey to show that children are being excluded from psychotherapeutic treatment, explicitly or implicitly. Especially essential facts like 'individual inner growth capacity', 'spontaneous impulse for development', 'being encapsulated', 'having complexes', 'in need of disengaging therapy' (to mention a few) are an indirect indication that children who lack all or some of these essentials are not only automatically excluded but can also run the serious risk of being subjected to unsuited treatment. Even if we were in complete control of the milieu of these children by placing them in a residential treatment center, the procedures referred to could still hardly help them, or not at all. They would even run the risk of disintegration, allowing their situation to deteriorate and their chances of a normal life to diminish.

The view that the child has complexes should also be differentiated. These are seldom found among the excluded group; the child has no problems, but is a problem.

This non-neurotic group is severely disturbed and presents difficulties in treatment. They are sometimes discarded, for convenience, dismissed as

15

psychopathic children. This frees them from criminological problems, but more especially from finding necessary treatment.

Others wish to deny severe disturbances. Out of compassion they often desperately try to account for them as neurotics and to treat them as such. This results in confusion, and consequently much hinders scientific progress. *Severer still is the damage done to children by wrong treatment.*

The Dutch psychiatrist Hart de Ruyter has a clear opinion about psychotherapy of children with severe behavior disorders: '1. Often psychotherapy departed from incorrect indications; 2. the current forms of psychotherapy proved inadequate for difficult children in residential treatment centers in many cases' (p. 4).

Redl and Wineman (1951, 1960[3]) and Redl (1966) who adopted their ego-psychological views from Aichhorn (1957) accordingly distinguished their pupils from children recovering by analytic treatment only, and adopted another course.

Most studies have been published on the subject of the heterogeneous group of neurotic children. Nearly all psychotherapeutic literature bears upon their treatment.

There is another group, heterogeneous as well. For lack of a better term, in this case too, we call the children belonging to this group: 'children with severe behavior disorders'. In the next chapter we shall attempt to distinguish some sub-groups. In other words, to consider what different 'treatment demands' are made within this group.

2. Structopathy as a sub-type of severe behavior disorders

1. NEUROTIC CHILDREN AND CHILDREN WITH SEVERE BEHAVIOR DISORDERS

From the discussion in chapter 1 we can progress to a division into two groups: neurotic children and children with severe behavior disorders. The second group is formed, as we have seen, by exclusion (not only theoretically) and as such only comprises those who do not fit in elsewhere. For the time being this group can be indicated somewhat negatively as children who have proved to constitute a serious problem as regards education. They can hardly be helped by existing psychotherapeutic methods of treatment if at all. Typical of this group is not only the fact that a psychotherapeutic approach is not effective because it is part-time, but also that the nature of the current therapies, such as psychoanalytic and non-directive approaches, is unsuited for them, as practice proves. On the one hand, as we have said before, these children *have* no complexes or problems, but *are* a problem.

Besides, it is hard do enlighten them fairly rationally regarding their own situation. Even if this could be achieved, the result would be zero. On the other hand, they lack spontaneous inner growth capacity, and in a non-directive climate anxiety, acting-out and similar phenomena increase, owing to a greater loss of 'the self', instead of the symptoms decreasing with greater self-realization. The disturbance lies deeper, more central, during or before the development of their personality and of their ego, which is to function as a centralizing factor. That is why the picture is more diffuse, the disturbance more widespread in all personality aspects; their chances are slighter, they have fewer sound link-ups, it is difficult to establish a therapeutic relationship. Disintegration or rigidity, rather than encapsulation, is imminent.

Instead of adopting two completely recognizable distinct groups, it is more realistic to try and place them on a continuum. We have already discussed children who cannot be helped *yet* and who have no problems *yet*. This means that not only are there a number of borderline cases, which within their own group verge very close on another, or are just in between, but with adequate treatment, at least some of the children in the group of severe behavior disorders might be moved on this continuum towards a more liberating treatment. This might mean that they can indeed be treated psychotherapeutically, if necessary, after a given period of other treatment, to be indicated later on. Our aim is rather to indicate that in that case they need a real, liberating education.

We reject therefore an absolute contrast between the two, and prefer polarity. The poles of the continuum represent the extremes: on one pole we find the child with very slight behavior disorders, on the other the child with whom a relationship is hardly possible. The border between both groups is somewhere on the continuum. This is a real division, justifiable according to suitability for liberating approach, yet this border is not an absolute division, in view of the assumed possibility of transfer from one treatment type to the other. There will be children who can be clearly placed on one side or other of the continuum and thus clearly approaching the treatment type (therapeutic and sociotherapeutic) of that pole. Other children however will be situated 'somewhere in between'. Diagnostics for treatment is more difficult in this case. One of the main problems facing us is that of the 'intermediate' children, from whose behavior one simply cannot infer the appropriate treatment, because both 'encapsulation' and mild forms of 'disintegration' may manifest more peripherally similar phenomena.

The more the child approaches the 'behavior disorders pole', the less chance there is of a shift to the other pole and a consequent crossing of the 'border', not only because the distance is greater quantitatively, but also because possibilities are smaller qualitatively. Experience mainly with this group may result in rejection of the idea of relatively smooth transitions, because the essential differences, the dissimilarity in quality, seem too great. In connection with follow-up treatment of a large group of children Robins (1966) states 'we have specified childhood patterns which appear to predict sociopathic personality in adults' (p. 309). Serious cases of 'sociopathic personality, antisocial reaction, psychopathic personality' (Robins, p. 1) are involved. These have a poor prognosis, if they belong to the syndrome she describes and comply with 'criteria for the diagnosis of sociopathic personality' (Robins, p. 342–343), because they are in danger of not being 'movable' on the continuum. The question remains to what extent, for these cases too, help will be possible in the future, especially because Robins' efforts enable a clear-cut diagnosis even at an early age. Robins' slight pessimism would only be justified if real treatment had taken place.

Heredity and brain damage

The foregoing presents another aspect which may be typical of the group with severe behavior disorders. True, it is different from the principle of treatment type, but it is closely related as regards scope and nature. We refer to the conventional and ever-recurring concept of hereditary psychical deviation. Without going into all the historical ins and outs of this concept, it can be said that nowadays the likelihood of psychic disturbances for reasons of heredity and predisposition has been mainly replaced by the idea that milieu has been the prevailing pathogenic factor. On the other hand, brain damage is increasingly mentioned as a contributory cause.

Let us start with the latter: among a considerable number of children who are closer to the 'severe behavior disorders' pole, organic defects are found, while at the same time a connection can be proved to exist between these defects and disturbed mental functioning and behavior.

If brain-damaged functioning is to be related to severe behavior disorders, accurate analysis of facts and possibilities and awareness of prejudices are needed. Let us now deal with this matter briefly to elucidate our point of view and return to it later on with more extensive and concrete examples. We do not accept a complete causal connection between organic defects and severe behavior disorders. Nor do we deny that there might be some connection. The former suggests the inevitability that organic defects must necessarily lead to severe behavior disorders. In our opinion this view rests on an irresponsible reversal of propositions: a child with deviating behavior a has symptoms x, y and z. If symptoms x, y and z are found in a child, he must exhibit deviating behavior a, right now or later. We reject these determinist ideas, although we do not wish to deny the possibility of a connection: deviating behavior *may* arise, but not necessarily. Only when it occurs, should one consider a causal relationship. Especially where slighter organic deviations are concerned, is it debatable whether severe behavior disorders or neuroticism will result. One might even suggest that development, which had been free from specific problems and had led to social adjustment, need not automatically have been exempt from slight organic disfunctions. Interesting in this connection is what Stemmer says about the choreatiform syndrome among children: 'At primary schools

19

only about 46% of the boys, whose ages ranged from 7 to 11 years, showed no trace of these involuntary movements' (Stemmer, p. 59).

If the problem is approached from a different angle, the connection between severe behavior disorders and organically defective functioning is often too strongly denied or ignored in our view. This has three causes.

Firstly the idea that severe behavior disorders are invariably linked up with emotional neglect in the milieu. The fact is overlooked that when personality development is in serious danger, this may also be caused by cognitive defects. The connection between resulting ego-disturbances and neurological disfunctions (Giffin, p. 75–97) can be demonstrated. In that case there is a relationship between cerebral disfunctions and learning difficulties (Myklebust, p. 1–15) and we must keep in mind that a primary learning difficulty also threatens acquisition of a normal way of life and personality development.

A second cause is the supposition that children who really suffer from primarily emotional disturbances, have been affected by milieu alone. This is possible, but thorough research will have to prove that the opposite cannot be the case, particularly to achieve correct treatment planning.

A third cause, the problem of diagnosing slighter neurological deviations, is removed when research apparatus and neuropsychological aid are perfected. 'The conventional neurologist often fails to find significant deviations in patients in whom the primary complaint is an inability to learn', Vuckovich (p. 30) states, after a previous remark: 'To provide depth in the analysis of maturation of the central nervous system, the conventional neurological approach must be extended to include test materials for developmental assessment' (ibid, p. 17). This can only be achieved in collaboration with the neuropsychologist, the author states with reference to Gesell. 'It was the psychologists and educators who stressed that an organic brain dysfunction, i.e., neurological disabilities, were present' (ibid., p. 36).

Neglect

The influence of milieu as a factor in a positive and negative sense, with respect to the presence and origin of both neuroticism and severe behavior disorders is bound up with the concept 'neglect'. A more detailed discussion of this topic is postponed till chapter 3. We shall now only deal with 'milieu' in connection with biological defect.

Severe behavior disorders solely based on milieu influences were not fully dealt with above.

Besides this, we discussed the relationship between milieu and organic defects developing into severe behavior disorders or not. Since milieu is a human i.e. free factor, as opposed to what is biologically determined, morals play an additional role. This leads to another question, viz. to what extent is there a failure for which the milieu is to blame?

This aspect of guilt is implicitly included, not so much intentionally as gradually, in the milieu factor, as is apparent from the emotive connotation of the term 'neglect'. If we start from the divisions of 'milieu alone' $\leftrightarrow$ defect and milieu' and 'milieu guilty $\leftrightarrow$ milieu not guilty', some differentiations can be made:

- If we can neither demonstrate nor suppose any biological defect at all, milieu must be the only cause; it may be a matter of guilt and if so, the degree may vary.
- A defect in the child appears to be the cause of a problem, whilst milieu is contributory; who is then guilty?
- A deficient child has severe behavior disorders, and, as far as the milieu is concerned, it is not only impossible to ask who is morally to blame but also impossible to speak of failure in up-bringing.

In the third case – which occurs very frequently – there is for instance a normal family milieu with a reasonably educational climate. Some children thrive, whereas one gives more and more serious problems and gradually becomes unmanageable. It could theoretically be a 'rejected' or 'unwanted' child. However if thorough examination gives no clues in this direction, but, on the contrary, reveals increased efforts to 'win' and educate the child, and there are also organic deficiencies, e.g. due to a birth trauma, this cannot be primarily put down to mistakes on the part of the milieu.

RD 3–4 (see appendix 1), a boy, is the fourth and youngest child from a good family. He is a rhesus child, exsanguinized several times, but due to an administrative mistake not until a very late stage. Choreatiform hyperactivity and frequent drops in energy now he is older indicate that subcortical damage has developed. He was a restless baby and a difficult infant. His behavior is so wild and thoughtless that he is in constant danger of getting hurt. But he is also inclined to hurt other people and damage things around him. The M. gives him every opportunity to move about and explore freely, but her presence is always needed. This gives more and more problems. The child is uncontrollable, all normal educative means fail, he only becomes wilder and more aggressive.

On the advice of others the M. leaves him for a short while in the garden when he is 3 ; 2 together with other infants. She instantly loses sight of him and although an immediate search is made, he manages to run straight into a truck. In hospital he is in a coma for 24 hours and he is nursed for a severe concussion of the brain for five weeks. His behavior is such that he has to be tied up and he escapes three times nevertheless.

After this period in hospital he develops measles and gets encephalitis. In the child

21

guidance clinic where he stays afterwards, the lady psychotherapist declares him unfit for treatment. Back home the head of the kindergarten manages to keep him for a period of six weeks, thanks to the efforts of all teachers. When this is no longer possible and the M. gets exhausted, sociotherapeutic help is called in.

Obviously the family was unable to supply adequate up-bringing and education for this child. But can a family be expected to cope with all this? (We use the word 'can' in this respect not only in the sense of 'being able', but also 'may'). Are parents justified in turning their family into a treatment center at the expense of their other children and thus putting an end to a normal pedagogical environment? Nor can foster parents automatically solve these problems.

Conclusions and summary

It will be clear from what has been said in this section that brain damage is not neglected, though it is not considered the only causal factor. Severe behavior disorders resulting from other causes are also taken into account. We are not defeatist when in treatment and up-bringing we take impediments resulting from organic deficiences into account, nor are we pessimistic as therapists. We must be realistic and willing to give adequate help. Otherwise sociotherapeutic work would become mere fighting of windmills. We do not consider the biological fact as an inevitability, as will be clear from our aims for sociotherapeutic treatment. For the socio-therapist is by profession the most optimistic member of the staff, though not unrealistic. More often than not therapeutic practice shows that milieu may also have a positive effect on organically defect functioning, even if this seems a pronounced disease. Our sociotherapeutic treatment rests on these views concerning milieu and though there are many cases where its immediate influence is questionable, the following is perhaps a singularly clear example.

RV 3–1 suffers from grand-mal epilepsy. Behavior disorders occur at home and at school. A vicious circle is the result and in spite of anti-epileptica, the patient deteriorates, in behavior, non-susceptibility and frequency of attacks. Before long he has two attacks a day and is put in a residential treatment center. The staff neurologist there stops his medicine, in accordance with his view on the relation between epilepsy and milieu and his impression of the therapeutic climate in the center. The boy has been there for 26 months now without having had any attack.

In short, children with severe behavior disorders are, to our mind, those who cannot be approached in a non-directive and permissive way. For that reason they are 'at a pole of the continuum', marked by great difficulty in entering a therapeutic relationship. The cause will be a severe disturbance in personality development, even severe hindrance or delay in the development of the personality itself. A biological component is not an absolutely necessary cause, but often proves to be basal. The milieu, with its psycho-physic and psychical powers always plays a part, sometimes a leading one, sometimes a minor part in forming the over-all picture.

2. FORMALISTIC AND POORLY-STRUCTURED CHILDREN

Polarities

Experience with children with severe behavior disorders has made us distinguish between two types. A normally developing child can be characterized by great formalistic flexibility (Rousseau used the expression 'perfectibilité' even in his days, and, from the actual development point of view, by a steady increase in structural refinement. Deficiencies in the former lead to rigidity, which for instance manifest themselves in formalistic behavior. Deficiencies in the latter lead to lack of structure: functions, if they do develop, seem to lead an incoherent and detached existence of their own, so that any outside pressure may cause this incoherent mass to fall to pieces. Educators, concerned with up-bringing these children have always sought to 'mould' the second group and to 'prize' the first group open. It may sound rather crude to talk of 'prizing' children open, but this gives a fairly good picture of what actually takes place. In addition we need another term to avoid confusion with the non-directive approach applied to neurotic children, also including formalistic types as indicated when discussing Slavson.

Let us refer once more to the previously mentioned criterion, in the following terms.

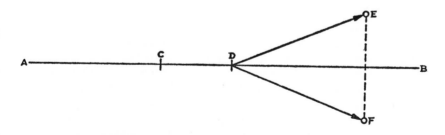

A and B are the poles of the continuum. A stands for the slightly neurotic child, and therefore also borders on normal education. Round B the child with extreme behavior disorders is situated. At worst an imaginary child, with whom hardly any or no therapeutic relationship can be realized. Between C and D is the transitional area between neurotic children and children with severe behavior disorders. Here we find children who seem to have severe behavior disorders, but who in fact turn out to belong to line A–C, as regards treatment. Children who react inadequately to non-directive treatment, so that they should perhaps be approached as between D and B. Finally the children who belong to this transitional area after successful treatment in group D–B; from there they return to normal up-bringing, either directly or by way of additional treatment A–C.

The points E and F mark the distinguishing dimension within the group of children with severe behavior disorders, discussed in this section. E indicates a child of extremely poor structure, whereas F represents the very rigid type of child. Therefore the sub-groups can be situated somewhere on the arrows DF and DE.

Witkin dimension

Line EF represented on the continuum is also met outside intuitive educative experience as a psychological dimension among authors who study the analysis and structuring of visual observation as a criterion concerning differences in observation and cognition. Witkin mentions a number of experiments he makes to establish on which point of the continuum field-dependency/field-independency his testees can be placed (1962, p. 36 ff). In order to ascertain the influence of this function on the development, a number of children are subjected to an extensive personality and milieu examination. He does not only aim at information concerning children who can be placed at the extremes of his continuum: 'a final objective was to make a careful study of intermediate children' (p. 229). Although in this study we compare Witkin's continuum with line EF, (being a vertical on a horizontal axis, on which extremes have already been fixed) we can only employ the extreme Witkin types.

For on sections CD, AC and the line not indicated to the left of A where the non-problematical children belong on our continuum, 'Witkin-verticals' could also be projected, indicated by E^1F^1, E^2F^2, E^3F^3. Inversely proportionate to the higher degree of development, the spread between the extremities diminishes the more one proceeds to the left of the continuum. If the Witkin-dimension were fully represented, it would form a trapezium on its side F^3E^3EF, with F^3E^3 representing the short and EF the long parallel sides.

24

The 'limitedly differentiated children' are the easiest to characterize 'perhaps because limitedly developed individual complexity permits less varied forms of integration' (p. 262).

These children with a 'low level of differentiation' turn out to be children with 'poorly-articulated experience, undeveloped self-concept, limited resources, and poorly-developed controls', or children with 'confused and poorly articulated experience, unclear self-concept, and severe impulse disturbance; their efforts are unrealistic, unadaptive, and poorly directed'. The good scope for compensation which some children have, like power of verbal expression, does not enable them to obviate field-dependency. The better-developed function deteriorates into a technique in order to conceal the underlying deficiency as much as possible (p. 247–257). The field-dependent children therefore appear to have a conspicuous lack of articulated and coherent experience, poorly-developed self-concept and extremely poorly-developed controls. One might also say that their structuring of the situation and resulting self-structure, enabling a more developed and more controlled expressivity, are disturbed in the sense that a development of this spiral does not get going. These are poorly-structured children.

It is evident that many 'normal' well-developed children are found among the 'highly-differentiated children' (p. 231–247). Witkin gives one example of a severely disturbed child in this group (p. 244–247). It concerns a 'complex boy who illustrates a high level of differentiation in the context of severe personality disturbance'. This boy screens himself off by 'paranoid protective mechanisms'. Although superficial observation of his behavior, impulsive at times, may suggest a poorly structured child, thorough examination and observation show strong formalisation.

In the field of Witkin's studies, 't Lam (1965) examines a group of children with minimal brain damage who receive treatment in therapeutic institutes because of severe behavior disorders and learning difficulties at school. Into this experimental group all children treated within the scope of our study so far have also been included. With respect to what was stated concerning 't Lam's first factor (p. 146 ff.), it might tentatively be concluded that the subtests of 'block-design' and 'drawing' from a Dutch non-verbal intelligence test (SON) are representative of the differences in level of differentiation of the Witkin dimension. In practice children with high or low block design (also after 't Lam's research) are clearly distinguishable, assuming that partial disfunction and disharmonic intelligence structure are the case. Children with relatively low block-design proved to be poorly structured. Disturbed children with high block-design scores either belonged to the autistiform type or exhibited formalistic, compulsive behavior (sometimes more neurotic).

They are children who desperately try to block out defects in the sub-structure by way of rigid control from high-level functions and thus develop a neurotic superstructure.

Intelligence and behavior disorders

The Witkin-dimension provides a diagnosis of the intelligence-structure, necessary for appropriate handling of the cognitive treatment aspects in a more limited sense, and gives an idea of the state of the personality as a whole and of the type of treatment. If intelligence is not taken purely as a license for scholarly success and later for choice of school, but as an aspect of personality closely related to the core, and also determining the development of every individual personality, qualitatively too, the foregoing will be clear. In this connection Redl and Wineman speak of the cognitive function of the ego (Redl; Wineman 1951) and indicate how non-functioning in this respect causes disturbed social-emotional development.

Inclusion of the intelligence structure in the personality is not intended to supersede the social-emotional aspects, but rather to provide a more realistic total picture and to illustrate contributory causes of defects in social-emotional development. The problem of disturbed development and growth is viewed rather from the standpoint of perception, the latter being taken as the tangent plane of the child and his world, as the possibility of realization in the world and consequent self-realization. Knowledge and learning, interwoven with the social-emotional aspect, are a self-formulating pattern of life, a structuring of what presents itself to the child, leading to increased structural differentiation of the individual himself. This hypothesis, with its origin in therapeutic practice and closely-related psychological research, can be taken as a working hypothesis, and can help to shape the course of treatment. In this sense it will be discussed in full in chapter 5.

3. STRUCTOPATHIC CHILDREN

We have made a distinction between children showing lack of structure and formalistic children. When we elaborated on this, we concentrated most on the first, because classification in this study is intended to specify which sub-group was examined as regards potential treatment. This is the group of poorly structured children, so further discussion of the children characterized as being formalistic is not necessary, save for a single remark.

26

Extreme rigidity and formalism are characteristics of the autistic child. The line D–F can indicate children with slight autistiform traits down to severely autistic children.

An essential question, because in practice theoretical distinctions intermingle, is where to place the psychasthenic child (with severe compulsion neuroses). Since in this case, too, the total personality is characterized by formalism, we shall first have to branch off from line D–F. However, since some children with a lack of structure sometimes have compulsion as an attendant symptom, this 'off-shoot' should be situated somewhat closer to line D–E. As far as the group with severe behavior disorders is concerned, we need not bother to what extent the compulsive phenomenon as a symptom also occurs in the group of neurotic children.

A treatment type primarily needs a description of behavior phenomena and the crystallization of a demand for treatment. We do not intend to depart from this, in fact our description in the next chapter will be based on it. We feel that the above theoretical discussion was necessary, if only to recall the familiar facts. We intend to give a tentative description of structopathy shortly, to conclude the classification in subgroups, but this will really only be an explanation of the term.

The fact that someone has severe behavior disorders, in that he is poorly structured is not a static condition. Something fatally dynamic occurred right at the start, when something went pathologically wrong, causing a primary discontinuum, seriously hindering structuring of the outside world and oneself. Disfunctioning makes itself felt in all genetically developing functions, on the differentiation principle, and so lack of structure should be seen as a pathological progression. To indicate the patho-genetic dynamics of this lack of structure, we employ the term 'structopathic children', in lieu of the description 'having severe behavior disorders of the poorly structured type.' This concept will be described in full in chapter 3 and a point-by-point summary will follow in chapter 4.

4. STRUCTOPATHIC SUB-GROUPS

In order to round this topic off, we can now give a preview of the divisions according to structopathy. Within the structopathic group we can make an additional differentiation based on a criterion found in practical treatment: the degree of sthenicity.

This polarity, also found outside this group, expresses itself in clearly marked behavior.

Sub-type: sthenic

In a group the sthenic structopathic child shows several striking tendencies: obtrusion, waywardness, bossiness, an implicit assumption that others can be used, aggressive and acting-out behavior. These children regularly cause tension and direct conflicts within the group. They are a constant source of worry, discussion and queries for the group workers. We have a shrewd suspicion that this type of child strongly resembles the second sub-type, as described by Witkin under the 'low level of differentiation': the child with 'severe impulse disturbance'.

Sub-type: asthenic

The asthenic child is far less conspicuous, in that he lacks obtrusion, because he 'swallows' the stress he experiences. Unlike their sthenic counterparts they display less 'arousal', which cannot only be established by observing the vitality evident in behavior, but encephalographically as well. (So here arousal is taken as a physiological concept, i.e. functioning of the reticular and thalamo-cortical system). It is assumed to bear some resemblance to Witkin's first sub-type among the children with a 'low level of differentiation'; children with 'poorly-articulated experience' and 'limited resources'.

These cases crop up less frequently in group discussions. As they cannot really cope with the stresses, they may fly into a rage when least expected (Redl; Wineman, 1951). A more indirect and delayed, so less frequent form of acting-out, may puzzle the group leaders because the tantrum bears no direct relation to the occasion. The members of the group will often react with amazement followed by rapid aggression or scorn; in both cases this just adds fresh resentment for yet another tantrum in the freshly-subdued child. Apart from these delayed major outbursts we also observe slight forms of aggression, mostly when the child notices the group leaders or primarily aggressive companions are not watching him too closely; this is somewhat incorrectly labelled 'stirring up trouble'. In this way tension and conflict in the group are created more indirectly.

Both sthenic and asthenic structopathic children suffer from too low a frustration threshold.

Sub-type: chaotic

A third sub-type can be derived from the group discussed above: children who do not even react with delayed acting-out, but who lead a more undirected existence. They are characterized not only by slight arousal, but also by an almost complete lack of intentionality. They just exist and because of their lack of structure they are exposed to any situation stimulus and react with increasing discomfort (by whining, grumbling, crying, complaining etc.), without clearly directing themselves at anything or anybody. They suggest a chaotic existence. To put it more accurately, their structopathy is not apparent, in that they clearly 'disintegrate' in given situations, or in a decreasing hold on the situation and themselves, but in that they are disoriented all the time. The fact that they are somewhat more formal and compulsive than the two sub-types of structopathic children mentioned previously, is a last means of self-protection. This characterization situates this group between the asthenic structopathic children and children with severe behavior disorders of the formalistic type. If, however, structopathy is their major problem and compulsion is of minor importance, we think it more correct to go on classifying them under the subgroup of structopathic children.

An educator with a positive attitude may still consider direct or delayed acting-out behavior a form of establishing contact. The third type within the subgroup of structopathic children now discussed can often be very irritating, because he does not even act or react negatively. When establishing contact he merely shows an increase of undirected discomfort. In this respect it is not only hard to diagnose treatment for the child as a border-line case within the group with severe behavior disorders, but great care should be taken too in distinguishing between this group and the regressive neurotic child in the neurotic group. Superficially both the neurotic and this structopathic child display lack of contact. The educator's reactions however will alter in course of time.

Quiet, withdrawn neurotic children are not annoying. That is why they are even found to be agreeable and welcome in class. The structopathic child is just the opposite. He is very disturbing and is rapidly rejected by his teacher and companions.

Differentiation diagram

Let us now extend our diagram with what we have just discussed.

D–E 1, 2, 3 is the area of the structopathic children. D–F 1, 2 the area of the formalists. A location closer to D or one of the other extremes indicates the degree of structopathy or formalism. Line E1 indicates sthenic, E2 asthenic and E3 chaotic structopathic children. F1 represents formalistic children, whereas F2 represents autistiform and autistic children.

This diagram is an extreme over-simplification of the real situation. Though there may be children who can be placed directly on one of the

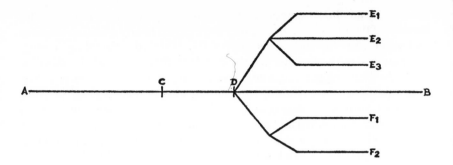

E-lines after thorough investigation and observation, there will be others who are somewhere between the lines. We have already discussed the transitional area (C–D), to which children who cannot clearly be included in A–C or D–E belong. In cases of diagnostic doubt only a tentative sifting of the treatment possibilities will provide clarity.

The diagram only indicates some groups essential to our subject. It refers to those children with primarily cognitive disturbances. Emotionally disturbed children, a heterogeneous group as well, have not been included.

Moreover, several other items should not be overlooked either when determining location. We have already discussed milieu as a contributory cause for occurrence of an organic defect. In as far as milieu was pathogenic, it may have been confusing, as the underlying patterns of structopathy were interwoven with superimposed traits of neglect, rejection etc. This may hamper positioning in the diagram. If a clear picture of the essential problems is to be obtained and adequate treatment facilitated thanks to positioning on the diagram, we must now determine how far behavior is a symptom of deficiency or a phenomenon resulting from residence in a treatment center.

In his discussion of social group work in the residential treatment center Maier states: 'In his group work practice within a residential treatment setting, the worker must clarify for himself which factors in his clients' behavior are related to complications that lead to placement and which are an outgrowth of the processes and circumstances of placement and institutional living ..... The worker has to be especially cognizant of the many hurdles associated with institutional placement and living' (Maier, 1965, p. 32). Redl and Wineman think these problems more acute in the initial period of placement. They distinguish a number of behavior categories in essentially pathologic behavior. These categories result from treatment shock, a phenomenon found among most children who arrive in a treatment project which challenges their former adaptability.

3. Structopathy as a disturbance type

1. BEHAVIOR

The type of disturbance represents a multidisciplinary description. But first and foremost it is a 'demand' for a specific approach. This 'demand' is bound up with behavior. Let us see what the parents have to say about it.

Parents' stories

From hundreds of talks with parents we have selected a few themes which occurred most frequently.

'We went out of our way, but it was no use, no matter how kind or stern we were. On the contrary, things are getting worse now he's getting older. And surely we should pay attention to our other children as well, shouldn't we?'

'She's not improving, whatever you say or promise. And when she is in one of her moods she seems to be deaf to the world'.

'My husband and I have had endless talks about it, we shouldn't ask too much of him, and especially keep cool and friendly. We've been trying hard to find ways of praising and rewarding him. But the moment you succeed in making a deal, things go wrong again. Still, he is not deaf; we asked the doctor'.

'I feel bad when I'm watching a T.V. program about difficult children. Were we so wrong? Surely, we'll have made our mistakes, but we sure did treat him just as well as our other children, or better!'

'Somehow I think she's bright, but if you see how clumsy she is, not learning or understanding anything after all ....'

'It wouldn't be too bad, if he were only so at home, but the neighborhood. He can't be handled in kindergarten either. I feel embarrassed when I take him home and then all these mothers watching me, for he's up to anything and a menace to any child'.

'We moved last month, just because of him, for we had a fine house.

But everybody was complaining like hell. The women next door went after him, but he's as slippery as an eel. Then there was this woman throwing stones at him, but he went one better throwing back. Then she saddled me with this child welfare guy! Just imagine'.

'He needs constant attention and even so he's never out of mischief. When my husband gets home in the evening I'm exhausted and then it's his turn to watch him, though he could surely do with a bit of rest himself. I've been taking pills for a long time now but it's no use, I'm on my last legs'.

Disturbed behavior

It would take volumes to record all our talks with parents. We can summarize the essence of those recurrent talks as follows:
1. The child is characterized by undirected hyperactivity, interrupted at irregular intervals by longer or shorter spells of relative calm.
2. The child is hypersensitive to stimuli and reacts to situational changes with motor unrest.
3. Contact can hardly be established with the child, who does not learn on the basis of experience.
4. He lacks duration in his relation to both persons and objects; he wanders around without concentration.
5. The child is soon frustrated and at times he panics unadaptedly for his age when there is no stress, as if he is threatened.
6. He hardly needs any emotional contact, except when he calms down, in which case contact on a primitive level and of a passive and tactile nature is necessary.
7. Because of his maladjusted behavior and rapid frustration, the child is always causing social conflicts, sometimes culminating in over-aggressive or destructive behavior, to the point of pseudo-sadism.
8. The child does not take long to fall into a heavy sleep and cannot be waked.

The following points are worth noting:
9. In most cases there is no more than one structopathic child per family.
10. Extensive milieu research in most cases gives no clue as regards neglect in the proper sense of the word.
11. When asked what is wrong with their child, parents, after having told their problems, on the whole appear to be of the opinion that the child lacks perception ('he fails to see it', 'it's as if she doesn't hear it' and sometimes 'he doesn't learn from pain or fear'). Next, that he lacks sufficient cognitive possibilities. ('Sometimes he seems to be mentally

defective', 'he doesn't understand', 'apparently she is not so quick on the uptake as the others', 'he doesn't learn from it').

Observation

With both individual and group contact, observation confirms the anamnestic behavior data. The child's failure appears to be closely related to lack of perceptual input. Not only does he have receptive and verbal weakness, but also makes the impression of inadequately analysing the situation and of being unable to clarify the situation himself or to participate adequately in what is going on. Cognitive failure is apparent. The child does not suffer emotionally.

The situation when 'authority' (father, mother, teacher, group leader) remonstrates with the child upon his failure is highly rewarding for the therapist. If the child is not in a state of hyperactivity and can be made to direct his attention to the adult, he looks at him with sincere amazement. The situation – which has occurred quite often before – makes him instinctively look meek, and for the adult's sake he is willing to promise various forms of amendment. The adult on his part however cannot help feeling uncomfortable because he figures, he is attempting the impossible: the child does not know what it's all about. He cannot bridge the gaps to his past.

2. DIAGNOSES

Neurological

'The afferentions, which are received by the nervous system in the optic, proprioceptive and tactile systems have become false and insufficient because of the diskinetic motor system, with which the child moves in the world around him', Prechtl states (1963, p. 11) concerning the child with the choreatiform syndrome. This preamble to neurological defects on the basis of structopathic development is not incidental, since with almost all structopathic children under treatment the choreatiform syndrome (whether or not complicated by other forms of brain damage) was diagnosed by the neurologist. It may vary in extent; it may even amount to chorea minor. To avoid any confusion the following must be said: not all children in whom choreatiform syndrome is diagnosed achieve structopathic development.

All structopathic children suffered from subcortical damage shortly before, during or after birth. The anamnesis reveals for instance pyloro-spasm, anoxia, asphyxia or xerosis.

Some suffered from neurotoxical damage at a later stage of develop-ment. At the same time many of them had complications: encephalitis, toxoplasmosis or commotio cerebri. Some were found to have disturbed reflexes, dilated ventricles and epileptiform EEG's.

The disturbance mainly affects perception, as indicated by Prechtl. 'These are children who can see, but whose ability to translate what they perceive into meaningful action is impaired – who can hear, but whose ability to translate what they hear into acceptable social behavior is minimal' (Cruickshank in his foreword to Haring and Phillips, p. VII).

Apart from perception another factor plays a role. It concerns the way and extent of directness in the process of perception, viz. in the tangent plane of subject and world.

Organic deficiency causes disturbances in concentration (Prechtl, p. 11). These may be due to decreases in consciousness or drops in energy. The sensorial and motor anomalies mentioned may be more serious in individ-ual cases owing to a specific defect. Sometimes slight sensorial-aphatic phenomena may be diagnosed. Motor disturbances are of course found in all cerebrally impaired children, but in individual cases they may be of a more serious nature.

It is obvious that these senso-motor function disturbances also affect perception disturbances. Directly they act as complicating and hindering factors. Indirectly, they provide an insufficient basis so that intelligence factors, which are genetically late, can only have retarded or insufficient development. For that matter we know from neurological literature, be it not very differentiated, that brain damage may cause more complete personality disturbances. Asperger points to the significance of a normally developing function of perception, when speaking about children with postencephalitic disturbances: 'Die pädagogische Situation ist bei diesen Kindern deshalb so verzweifelt, weil sich bei ihnen keine Erfahrungen aus-bilden, die in die Zukunft weiterwirken würden – und Erziehbarkeit hat eben 'Erfahrungsfähigkeit' zur Voraussetzung' (Asperger, 1956[2], p. 116). 'The brain-damaged organism, as we know, is abnormally responsive to the stimuli of his environment, reacting unselectively, passively, and without conscious intent', Strauss and Lehtinen state, followed by: 'When such a hypervigilant organism – one whose reactibility is beyond his own control – is placed in a situation of constant and wide-spread stimulation, he can only meet the situation with persistent undirected response' (Strauss; Lehtinen, 1958[8], p. 129). Disturbed perception and cognition may eventually lead to a 'catastrophic reaction' (Goldstein, 1939, p. 36–37; also see Goldstein, 1942), suggesting a more complete personality disturbance.

Psychological

In chapter 2 we anticipated the investigations of Witkin and 't Lam. Poorly-structured children especially appeared to have cognitive disturbances. Their perception development is hindered.

Nooteboom examines children with the choreatiform syndrome, in collaboration with Prechtl. She ascertains learning difficulties in these children. These hamper school performance. But at the same time they limit personality development (Nooteboom, 1967, p. 1 and p. 44–45). Since all structopathic children suffer from the choreatiform syndrome – and not the other way round – these data are of importance to us. Although it is evident that structopathic children will vary slightly as regards behavior, their psychological data do in the main correspond. These can be summarized as follows.

They have a disharmonic intelligence structure, in which the functions of visual analytic structuring perception and of conceptual-motor structuring have comparatively weak development.

This could be described as attention pathology, characterized by a strongly fluctuating concentration, as shown in the Bourdon-Wiersma-test by greatly varying amounts of time needed for one line and many omissions (also in groups).

The children have a poorly developed, poorly integrated personality with a highly diffuse Gestalt-perception, great volatility, lack of substance and poor social-emotional development.

Visual analytic perception proved not to be relatively poorly developed in some cases. This was however the case with efferential structuring, in other words enabling variations while the concept is simultaneously kept constant. We cannot account for this; in this field further research is needed.

The report of the psychological examination not only mentioned a divergence in the time needed per line, ranging from 11 to 53 seconds as to the B–W, this test often had to be stopped because the child got so frustrated that further continuation was undesirable.

The personality examination (Rorschach, CAT, Sapat) failed to indicate emotional problems or repressions. Striking was the high percentage of diffuse G-answers, too low an F% and extremely low F + % and a complete lack of B's and color-shocks. Some quite intelligent children had a high percentage of O's, which we found strange, and remote from reality.

35

Diagnostically speaking, the disturbance type is a picture of the personality, and phenomenologically speaking it is a demand. The latter will be dealt with at the end of this section.

Integration of multi-disciplinary data

In the first two sections of this paragraph the basic material for this disturbance type was given. We must now arrange this and discover how it all links up.

The most striking neurological datum is the choreatiform syndrome. This motor disturbance can be traced back to disturbance of brain functioning. Psychological examination ascertains insufficient differentiation of perception. At the same time concentration disturbances are reported, which function as a strangely autonomous process. The connection of the latter with the neurological deficiency is clear. The sociotherapist observes an irregular attention span. Besides there are those curious moments of calm between the periods of hyperactivity. In both cases contact with the child is difficult. The child does not learn, and if he does, with difficulty: not only in school situations, but also in and from everyday life. It is not difficult to grasp the connection between these observation data and the psychological data. Nor is it difficult to establish an interrelation between the data from the several disciplines. However, the step from this to really complete treatment was not so simple. Therapists ran aground when trying to combine directions for treatment from the different disciplines: amphetamine (neurology), concentration training (psychology, often used as training in test-items), placement in an environment free from stimuli (therapy).

In all this only part-time treatment can be realized. We are still faced with the child in full-life situations. Never fear! Parents will be counseled concerning neurotic children: be kind and tactful, let the child behave in his own way. This kind of treatment will scarcely yield any result. The really structopathic children, who are serious cases, will go from bad to worse.

This sort of teamwork does not go beyond noting each other's findings and views. Real integration will not be effected. Departing from the time-honoured dictum 'that the whole is more than the sum of all the parts' a more complete idea of the disturbance will have to be created. The different disciplines are only part of a major plan. This new concept, born out of fusion, will be a view on the person's functioning and development as a whole. What is specific about being deviant? In what way can milieu be adapted?

Discontinuous existence

Structopathic children suffer from the choreatiform syndrome to a serious degree. Their motor system manifests irregular shocks, caused by irregularities in energy supply. But how can we account for disturbed concentration, diffuse perception and the inability to learn from experience? The disturbed energy supply does not only act on the motor system but also on the consciousness. The structopathic child suffers from an insufficient, viz. discontinuous attention span and from distractability. He leads a discontinuous existence, which in terms of the outside world means first of all getting fragmentary information and realisation.

We have in mind a situation other than psychological time, in that it can be subdivided into quantums. The discontinuous existence described in this section is still prior to psychological duration, just because time quantums stop. In a genesis disturbed in this way, an important aspect of spatial time – the ability to regulate – does not develop spontaneously. The process causing the biological rhythms, which function in the organism, to be synchronized with the temporary regulations offered or imposed by the environment does not get going, because the badly needed information from the environment is only conveyed in snatches and is therefore inaccurate.

In the terms of the Dutch author Hugenholtz the defect is said to function in the manner of experiencing vital time. Time makes the parts into a whole, the phases into a course, the tones into a melody. It makes one phase succeed another. Leading a discontinuous existence in the world is based on a biological defect, which prevents the continuity, as described by Hugenholtz, from developing. So this is different from what he calls discontinuity of animal time, discontinuous, momentary, concentrated time. This is of a higher order, for later, genetically speaking, 'animal time is superimposed on vital time', or a modification of it. Especially memory pictures, which are peculiar to animal time, do not develop spontaneously. From the point of view of developmental psychology, the disturbance pervades primary perception and experience. The linking element, constituting a person's basis, core and unity, does not function properly. No integration develops.

This discontinuous existence could be described as unconnected pieces of 'now', of a loose structure because of regular interruptions in attention or a complete lack of attention. There is no link and connection between 'this concrete experience' and former similar or different experiences, or – at best – an inadequate though very fragile connection develops to bridge the gaps, but lacking is the link between past and present, put into play when a picture from the past is recalled. The lamentation: 'it's just as if they've never done (heard, seen) it before' is an unintentional representation of the problem. In addition visual perception, in so far as this does function intentionally, remains diffuse and superficial, unlike in normal development. In that case analysing perception functions as early as four years of age (Nickel, 1967).

Insufficient analysing and structuring of the situation makes it impossible for the child to handle it. He is thrown off his already unstable balance. It is like walking through a thick fog, in which a sudden collision may occur; this cannot be anticipated, because it cannot be timed.

Discontinuity in conscious existence, pertaining to his world, is fatal for the structopathic child. Information, if it penetrates, is only experienced as arousal. It is not understood to be information and therefore not assimilated and integrated. If he is in such a state, the child experiences hyperactivity or a drop in energy. In either case sensible manipulation of the world is out of the question. Besides, he will not be able to act – by giving structure – on the basis of a concept.

Information intended for the child, (this is not only verbal information but also perception of behavior in its widest sense, the ability to make a structure out of a situation) may be given when he is 'absent'. And so there is no information. If the child pays sufficient attention, he is brought into contact with something for the first time. However, if he is to get a clear perception of structures, meanings, wishes and expectations regarding his behavior – notably in connection with a rise of level – the information in question will have to be regularly available. Learning, in this case 'learning to live' or 'getting to know life' is possible on the basis of experience: in a given situation a child can achieve adequate behavior because he has been in the same situation many times before and has 'learned'. He sees through a social structure and he can detach the behavior of others out of a total, and therefore understand, because he has often been in that situation. This is exactly the problem of the structopathic child: he may occasionally get some information, thanks to a healthy moment and a clear approach, but it is of little use to him. Neither at the moment it is given, because the past, the experience, is lacking, nor at a later stage because then he would have to bridge too many gaps.

Failure to present the past especially concerns visual and acoustic inability of recollection. In those cases where motor disturbances are not apparent, motor-kinesthenic recollections may function. Redl and Wineman note that there is only this very primitive link with the past, when taken in the sense of 'using previous satisfaction images as resource' (1951, p. 115).

Defective functioning as described above also sheds light on an essential part of deviating behavior in the sense of limited and hindered humanization. Historicity, a human characteristic, is running a serious risk. With this we do not mean 'historic consciousness', but its foundation, which makes it possible to create memory-pictures. Even more difficult than the development of a link with the past, causing historicity to begin, because the present is directly related to the past, is the genesis of a link with the future. During the development of the average infant, creative phantasy comes into being, which 'serves to help him overcome the common fears and problems of childhood' (Fraiberg, p. 27), because this function enables planning in the near future, but only after and on the basis of already functioning memory pictures. Next 'openness of perception' (Schulman, 1966) appears to be indispensable for creativity. Openness supposes that the 'perceiver views the world from many different vantage points in a playful manner' (ibid. p. 89). The perception of the structopathic child lacks both full functioning and flexibility.

This new functioning is studied especially with the aid of creative play. It will be clear that creative phantasy has proved in practice not to develop in structopathic children, or hardly so, and will function very poorly. At an age when normal children have independently carried out creative group play for some years, structopathic children have the greatest difficulty in reaching a planning, even with the help of others. Working it out in play at first requires constant help and is then often limited to a couple of minutes.

The problems involved are fundamentally different from those described as 'communication disturbances'. The life of a structopathic child has not been made so unsafe that it is only possible by the grace of what threatens him. Primarily the structopathic child is subjectively threatened by his disfunctioning precreative perception. The more so since milieu does not threaten, because a secondary developmental disturbance in the shape of neurotization does not play a part. Treatment of this aspect with various forms of play and manual expression does not aim at switching on a fixed function anew as a means of deneurotization, but rather is partly aimed at initial development.

Primary learning disturbance

The discussion of disturbances in perception, observation and cognition, will also bring learning difficulties at school to mind; either right at the start of the primary school as a form of immaturity, or as a more or less extensive partial disturbance in learning at school. This is only partly correct, because only then do a considerable number of children with this type of disturbance fail in this way because of their defect.

The structopathic children examined and treated are characterized by a very limited ability to learn. When we speak of learning disturbance, this is primarily a disturbance in learning to live, which hinders total development right from the start, chiefly from the moment that the child starts exploring on his own.

Later when he enters school, learning disturbances in a didactic sense will develop as well, on the basis of similar defects and past unadapted learning behavior. The new series of disappointing experiences at primary school as an extra disturbing factor may also show how advisable it is to start treatment well before the beginning of that period.

In short, structopathic children are seriously handicapped in their ability to learn. 'The possibility for brain-injured children to misunderstand a given situation is great because of the unique perceptual characteristics' (Cruickshank, 1967, p. 149). This defect is based on a disharmonic intelligence-structure, disturbances in concentration, senso-motor deficiencies, disturbance in their relations with and focus upon the world, which causes them to lead a fragmentary existence, and discontinuity, preventing links with past and future to develop.

This discontinuity also causes a disturbance in experiencing time and in the ability of realizing duration. Therapeutically speaking, the latter is especially important: it is a new impediment to progress, because any training will only be effective if it has a certain duration. Instead of being able to employ function training as such, this must first of all be utilized to extend the short spells – sometimes no more than a few minutes – of attention. An advantage is that this training can at the same time be used to regulate the discontinuous cerebral energy supply.

The 'demand' in the disturbance type

The disturbance type is fundamentally characterized as a demand from a phenomenological point of view: a demand for a specific approach. It is actualized in behavior. Diagnostics can accentuate it, if the demand scrutinizes the data.

Finally it constitutes the transition from disturbance type to first-grade strategy. In other words: it causes the coherence in the sociotherapeutic treatment type. What demand do structopathic children make to sociotherapists? If we could formulate this demand on their behalf, it would run as follows:

'Structure situations for me and restructure them instantaneously, so that if you present them clearly:
- I can make out some structure,
- I can lead a structured existence and function for a while,
- this makes me experience a better, more pleasant and more continuous existence,
- I want to return and get motivated to such an existence,
- in the course of time I myself can start giving some structure to my world,
- this allows me to get into a genesis of a structuring process, integrating both formally and content-wise (growth from within!)'

In chapters 5 and 6 we will discuss the answer, the first-grade strategy, and specifically one aspect of it, after giving brief description of it in section 5 of this chapter. In volume II of this study, the experimentally gained statistic data on the results of the treatment will be discussed.

4. DISTURBANCE TYPE: NOT EQUIVALENT TO ONE-SIDED DISCIPLINARY CONCEPTIONS

'Psychiatrists, neurologists, and pediatricians will recognize herein some of their most difficult, distracting, and likeable patients. Thus it is entirely possible that ... he might under various circumstances, be classified as brain-injured, or as one who demonstrates evidence of organicity or minimal brain injury. He might be viewed as emotionally disturbed; as having a home problem; as a psychopathological personality; as having a weak ego or lack of ego integration; as lacking inner controls and requiring a rigid, controlled, and highly structured environment; or as needing an environment which is warmly permissive. He could be regarded as needing immediate long-term residential treatment, or as not being amenable to psychiatric treatment' (1967, p. 16–17).

This quotation from Cruickshank demonstrates once again what problems arise if we do not start from sociotherapeutic treatment types. Though our view was discussed in the preceding section, we shall go into it once more. When new approaches and classifications are introduced, clarity is essential.

The notion 'structopathy' originated in sociotherapeutic thought. The word does not therefore apply identically to all groups of deviating people, formed on the basis of other classifications. In section 2 of the first chapter we expressed a different opinion from Cruickshank. As stated before, Slavson's opinion on treatment is more correct. In his opinion medical diagnostics is not decisive, but defect behavior is. Neuroticism and brain damage cannot be considered polarities, because other dimensions are involved. A brain-damaged child may be neurotic. Permissive, liberating treatment answers his 'question'.

The structopathic child suffers from the choreatiform syndrome. But not all choreatiform or hyperkineatic children are structopathic. If a neurological classification is used, then differences in the extent to which he is hyperkineatic or choreatiform are accepted. Stemmer, already quoted in chapter 2, section 1, establishes the choreatiform syndrome with 54% of normal schoolboys. A greater part of them has normal development and no difficulties in learning. By the age of 11 the phenomena disappear.

No more than 4% is in need of special help. A great part of this 4% benefits from special education. These could be 'Cruickshank'- or 'Prechtl'-children. Structopathic children suffer from a more severe form of this brain damage. They are primarily threatened by severe disturbances in their personality development. For this reason treatment should be primarily directed on the latter. Special education is of secondary importance. It will also be manifest that being structopathic entails more than neurology alone.

The question can also be approached from another angle. There are differences in the neurological disturbances of structopathic children which have caused sociotherapists to seek a common substratum. This was found in revealing identical biochemic deviations. Publications on this by the multi-disciplinary team will come out shortly.

5. THE FIRST-GRADE STRATEGY

This component of the 'structopathy' sociotherapeutic treatment type will be dealt with at length in the fifth and sixth chapters of this volume and in volume II. Let us conclude this chapter on the disturbance type with a brief summary of its components.

The structopathic child requires specific help in analysing all sorts of real life situations. This enables him to learn how to distinguish and handle structured entities. By giving structure to his world he gets structure both formally and regarding content.

If he is to have constant help, the child must spend some time in a specifically adapted residential treatment center. We shall deal with this extensively at a later stage. The first strategy in this center, and the therapeutic climate, will have to encourage structure-formation. This strategy boils down to intensified sociotherapeutic 'acting' in all real life situations, intended to supply the child with optimal possibilities to analyse and structure by methodical handling of those situations. This entails coming down to the child's level. Guided by the sociotherapist, group workers and teachers will continually have to handle and direct situations in such a way that the child can always apply and reach them. From a primitive start, the children themselves will receive an initial structure, by way of the positive experience of a more structured and meaningful world. And so they can benefit more and more from treatment, and develop themselves. So the task of the sociotherapist and his assistants shifts from more directive handling of situations and substitution of structured and structuring ego, to a more affirmative ability of entering a relationship. Let us hope that the following chapters elucidate these 'terms of reference'.

4. Other personality aspects of structopathic children: an empirical definition

The preceding chapter dealt with the type of the treatment. We only discussed the cognitive aspects of the children's personality. This is obvious since structopathic children primarily display cognitive disturbances.

A great part of this chapter is taken up with other aspects of the personality. In this respect it is therefore closely related to chapter 3, and so a defining summary of structopathic disturbance will not be given until the end of this chapter.

1. THE SOCIAL-EMOTIONAL ASPECT

Up to now we have only discussed cognitive disturbances, which might no doubt leave many of our readers with a feeling of frustration. We hope this will not give them emotional disturbances! But seriously: there are unfortunately many emotionally disturbed children. But structopathic children are not included in this class. The fact that they can be disturbed without being emotionally disturbed may be puzzling, and affect our line of thought.

Ever since Bowlby, experts and amateurs alike have taken a great interest in hospitalism and other syndromes, indicative of emotional neglect. The danger of generalization is imminent, especially when children show one or more symptoms, which might on the face of it suggest neglect. 'Man pflegt heute als 'verwahrlost' alles zu bezeichnen, was nicht so geraten ist, wie man es wünschen möchte. Untersucht man dann eine grössere Gruppe von in diesem Sinne verwahrlosten Kindern und Jugendlichen, so findet man, dass die Ursachen dieser Verwahrlosung zum Teil im Milieu, zum Teil aber in der Eigenart der Kinder selber liegen...!' (Moor, 1965, p. 87). The mistake made here is to overlook the second pole in the mother-child relation. If the child is unable to understand normal emotional approach, affirmation and limits, and if he is 'unteachable' in these primary patterns of life, treatment starting from another point of view has no result, or makes things worse. 'Over the last twenty years, almost all behavioral and learning problems in children in the United States have been treated as of pure emotional origin... The results of this approach have not been very encouraging' (Huessy, 1967, p. 130).

Backwardness of emotional development

Behavior observation and personality research prove that the emotional development of structopathic children has been severely retarded. Most of them appear to exist merely on the basis of comfort – discomfort. There is no further differentiation.

On this basis of underdeveloped 'emotional discernment', combined with increased irritability, the low frustration tolerance becomes apparent. There is hardly a trace of a nascent identification process. Sometimes there may be relationships with one or both parents, but on the level of the very young child. The imitation mechanism functions but is often hardly discernable from psychic contamination in a more pathological sense. Structopathic children have hardly any emotional norms, sometimes none at all. The most striking thing about these patients is that they hardly know how to deal with the affection offered. An affirming, permissive approach results in disintegration and chaotic development. Their capacity to perceive adequately and fully assimile the given affection, by which the child benefits, would seem hypothetically to be defective. The child lacks, as it were, 'emotional radar-apparatus', or this is so deficient that the signals cannot be converted into a useful picture.

This working hypothesis applies specifically to structopathic children only. Relevant literature and personal experience with children with other disturbances demonstrate that blocked affection caused by the milieu may be the origin of disturbed development and the fulchrum of our treatment. The impression of emotional neglect in not neglected structopathic children may be reinforced by complications when they are growing up. They may occasionally experience in a different manner the fact that they are different. This should not be interpreted as 'looking inward', but as some realization, on a vital level, of being approached differently from others. This perception, resulting from a malfunctioning personality, does not lead to genuine social insight and social learning. On the contrary, a mechanism is employed, which can be compared to rationalisation, and it resembles it the more as the child grows up and becomes more intelligent. Feelings of discomfort arising from frustrated perception are expressed (it is also typical of a primitive disposition that only feelings of discomfort can develop). As is normal for their age, not by crying but by talking: an 'explanation'

45

outside the child is sought after. This might for instance lead, in a projection examination, to verbalisation of having been wronged by and in the parental milieu, giving the impression of real neglect.

(AK6–1). This boy of 9;2 has been put down for treatment because of serious behavior problems and because 'he is a problem child' as the P. puts it. He is the second in a family of three children. The parents make a kind and normal impression. The M. is nervous and strained, is aware of it and agrees with the P's explanation that she's got into such a state because of the difficulties and worries concerning her son. The older brother and his younger sister do not present any problems, except that they sometimes become irritated by the behavior of the boy to be treated, or by the tensions he causes. Not only are there problems at home but the school has complaints as well, both as regards conduct and performance. The boy was said to be lazy, uninterested and careless, and inclined to make unnecessary mistakes. If a subject is to his liking and the material is offered orally, he proves to have absorbed and understood it exceedingly well afterwards. The teacher thinks that 'he's actually quite nice', but unmanageable.

The greatest problems however come from the neighborhood, where the boy is blamed – rightly or wrongly – for everything that happens. He has become an object of aggression to the woman next door and indeed he gets up to everything. His parents say that they are at their wits' end. Their son never seems to be out of mischief. They have tried everything, but to no avail, whether they were kind or strict. In the P's opinion the worst thing is that the boy, when lectured, looks as if he does not follow. In spite of everything the parents are of the opinion that their son may indeed mean well, but that he may be mentally defective. At any rate 'a young child in a bigger body'. When the CAT was taken the following story was told about the picture of the bears sleeping in and outside the cave: 'There were a daddy and a mummy bear who got a baby bear. When they went to sleep in the evening, the mummy and daddy lay down inside the cave. Daddy at the back. But the little one had to sleep outside. It was mighty cold that night! And the little bear was frozen to death, even before he had a name.' (Abridged version of the story, containing some agrammatisms and a great number of perseverations).

The CAT story could be a stock neglect-projection. All available channels were accurately used to discover earlier neglect, but there was no trace. Regular, unannounced visits to the family did not detect emotional neglect in the proper sense of the word. Neurological examination showed choreatiform hyperactivity, disturbed reflexes and petit-mal epilepsy. The anamnesis mentioned severely obstructed partus and some convulsions during the first years.

Once again it is evident how difficult it is to differ in diagnosis between neurotic reactions due to neglect and a social-emotional disfunctioning due to a more complete, organically-founded personality disturbance. In our view it remains typical that the more neurotic child *has* a neurosis, suffers from it and longs for another, more social situation: social hunger. The structopathic child has no neurotic aspects, but has remained primitive in a social-emotional respect. He is ignorant of, cannot cope with affection, avoids processes to establish social behaviour and only expresses dissatisfaction with his condition by non-specific feelings of discomfort, which he also expresses with hunger, pain and other unpleasant situations.

Another striking thing is that the child is amazed when a complaint is referred to later on: what he expressed only served as a form of packing to externalize diffuse discomfort.

Mixed cases and summary

Most of the structopathic children we treated come from normal families. But there are a few with whom some neglect has also played a part. If both structopathization and neglect were operative right from the beginning of postnatal development, it is often hard to ascertain which of the two components is most important. Yet this is crucial for a proper socio-therapeutic approach, as is clear from the problems involved in treating a structopathic infant, whose behavior was deviant before neglect had begun, following the death of the unmarried mother. More extensive discussion of the treatment follows in chapters 5 and 6, so suffice to say here that the sociotherapist in a case like this should try to steer clear of the rocks. Structopathy linked with organic deficiencies, resulting sooner or later in genuine emotional neglect, entails in a mixture of elements re-quiring contrasting treatment. For, whereas a highly affective, affirmative and permissive approach is necessary to break down neglect, more severe structopathization should be prevented by a structuring, possibly reg-ulating treatment, with the right amount of affection and affirmation, but not an excess (thanks to accurate planning). Diagnostics is here in a marginal area, notably between structopathy and sociopathy, and this area sometimes necessitates prolonged observation to decide the appro-priate treatment. Once we were thoroughly mistaken in a case of this kind. The anamnesis led us to carry out treatment for structopathy whereas after approximately six weeks the child we were dealing with proved to be sociopathic.

In short: structopathy can be distinguished from emotional neglect as regards symptoms, causes and treatment. Neglect may play a part, though it occurs far less than is superficially assumed.

Mesinger's question (1965) whether 'emotionally disturbed' and 'brain damaged' children (if the vagueness of both terms will satisfy the reader) can be treated in one and the same setting cannot therefore be answered without due reflexion. The foregoing will make clear that downright cases of neglect and structopathy cannot be treated similarly. Decisive in 'composite cases' is the approach to which the child (still) reacts favourably.

Backwardness of social development

The structopathic child's social development is greatly retarded too; sometimes it does not get going at all. This will not be surprising, if we consider what was said about emotionality, since both functions are still closely interknit at an early age, preventing a separate treatment of both aspects.

In our opinion the connection of the social-genetic defect with disturbed perception and cognition is closer, however. Analysis of the social situation is insufficient and discontinuous. We are of the opinion that defects in both social and emotional development of the structopathic child have one and the same cause: disturbed perception and cognition.

But are structopathic children unsociable? Frequently they are labeled so, especially by (frustrated) laymen.

The term unsociable has strong social connotations and cannot be applied to children. A child may be adapted to a possibly unsociable or antisocial milieu. Only if he went against the code of his own milieu could he be termed unsociable or antisocial. Yet something is wrong with the sociality of structopathic children. Complaints suggest strong ego-centricity, disregard of social 'rules' and also refusal to learn them. Other aspects are: improper behavior, refusal to consider the wishes of others, an inability to know whether something is permitted or not, a tendency to be very polite and kind at times, followed by a 'couldn't-care-less' attitude immediately afterwards, etc. It is also striking that the child, when lectured on violating the social rules chiefly gives the impression of amazement. Because of the situation and the feelings of the adult he is quite willing to look meek and to promise to behave better in future. But the adult gets the uncomfortable feeling that he is not only groping in the dark himself but that the child is entering unknown territory as well.

What was discussed above has been derived from experience with a great number of these children and we propose to term this aspect *pre-social*. Normal young children are found to show an implicit knowledge of belonging to something. Relationship which makes the child feel at home in his familiar social environment is taken for granted. This primary sociality has hardly developed in structopathic children, or not at all. This developmental inhibition is not the result of a shortage of input from the milieu. It is caused by disturbances in the ability to comprehend conceptualizations and in the possibility of development by way of absorption.

48

From what has been said above it follows that structopathic children have a *relation disturbance*. This is not a syndrome but a symptom. It is indeed found among very different treatment types. In so far as structopathic children also have relation disturbances, a genetic outlook is again preferred. We have already discussed how, because of disturbed perception, the social-emotional functions hardly develop, if at all. This seriously impedes establishment of either a cognitive or a conative relationship. In further development the diffuse disturbance will not only spread in all differentiating separate functions and continue to hinder integration, but also increasingly frustrating experience will, in the course of time, adversely affect the capacity and enthusiasm to enter a relationship, as in a descending arithmetical progression. Children who are seriously disturbed as to lack the capacity to enter a spontaneous relationship, are conspicuous at an early age, also because of the accompanying behavioral anomalies. Correct treatment, started at the age of 5 or 6, offers many more possibilities than an educative approach, not starting until or during adolescence. Not only is the whole latency phase available, but the child is at an age when the stranded development can still be stimulated in a fairly natural way. Only a short period of incorrect habitus development has preceded, and inadequate approach or treatment has not been able to do much damage. Practice shows that adequate sociotherapeutic treatment, if started in good time may lead to complete or considerable remedy of this disturbance.

2. EGO-DISTURBANCE

Gestalt psychology shows that there is a relationship between Gestalt perception and ego-development. Perceptive information and motor behavior cause experience in time and space. These processes constitute an intrinsic aspect of ego-development. Structopathy, non-integration, inability to structure a situation and to be structured can also be defined as a severe disturbance in the development of the ego. In the field of ego-psychology Redl and Wineman are the exponents of sociotherapy, because they employ it as the basis of treatment strategy (Redl; Wineman, 1951).
What makes this theory especially interesting and useful for the type of child we are concerned with, is the emphasis laid on the cognitive aspects of the ego, by which we mean both cognitive and selective functions. In this case too, disturbed perception and disharmonic intelligence are

related to a disturbed personality development. Failure of the ego as a human function explains phenomena like aggression and acting-out, especially as symptoms of acting. Without suggesting that the sub-group of structopathic children is identical to aggressive children, the former group does exhibit aggressive behavior, which may take the form of reaction and/or action. The former is closely related to the low frustration threshold and to the minimal control of the passions caused by a lack of personality structure, leaving hardly any scope for sublimation. The situation is a constant threat and is based on disturbed perception.

Aggression as acting – not re-acting – is still a debatable point. It is true that aggressive behavior cannot simply be seen as action, because there is no direct relationship between aggression and cause. In chapter 2, section 4 we discussed how the more asthenic type is characterized by a 'delayed release', mostly after impetus of stresses. We shall discuss how in the course of treatment a more indirect expression of frustrations, caused by incipient conscience development will be found in the more sthenic types who have primary reactions. As an introduction to a symposium on acting-out, Rexford (1966) gives a survey of the relevant views. Besides the interpretation of acting-out as a neurotic symptom, occurring in or outside the transference situation in adolescent or adult patients, and acquired by traumatic experiences in early childhood, she ascertains that several authors also mention a more primary form as a direct impulse. 'The development of impulse controls presents such difficulties for some little boys and girls that they become unmanageable ...' (p. 9). From Friedlander (1947) she derives: 'This formation shows the structure of the mind wherein instinctive urges remain unmodified and, therefore, appear in great strength, where the ego, still under the dominance of the pleasure principle and not supported by an interdependent super-ego, is too weak to gain control over the onrush of demands arising in the id' (Friedlander, p. 94). 'Acting-out is a puzzling phenomenon, which, I feel, deserves some elucidation. It is a characterologic disturbance and not a diagnostic entity. It may be a symptom of many pathologic conditions', Vass states (1965, p. 302), with her great experience in group therapy, thus taking not only a wider, but also a more correct view of this matter.

Some structopathic children sometimes have aggressive behavior, not to be related to outward or inward stress. These are sudden, often violent aggressions, sometimes of a somewhat sadistic nature. They can be the cumulation of a condition of hyperactivity, but they can also suddenly take place 'just like that'. Not only does profound analysis of the direct and preceding situations fail to elucidate the occurrence but the child himself cannot give an explanation afterwards either. Clearly this is not because the ability to verbalize is insufficient: the same child can indeed indicate a reason, however insufficient and highly subjective, after an aggressive reaction.

RD 3–4, 5;9, is very fond of RV 2–2 (7;6) in the group. He enjoys playing with her and he will watch her during play. Afterwards he starts stroking her hair and face, which she accepts with a smile. After these caresses have lasted one to two minutes – observed three times now – they stop and playing is continued.

This afternoon all of a sudden his expression changed while caressing her, and bright-eyed, with his mouth cruelly twisted he gripped her by the throat with both hands and tried to strangle her. Immediate action prevented things from getting worse. He was pale, tight-lipped and tense, and obviously somewhat exhausted. The same once happened after he had squeezed his hamster to death.

3. DEVELOPMENT OF CONSCIENCE

Considerable learning difficulties (habituation), causing social-emotional blockages (social sense of norms and identification) and disturbed development of the ego, impede the development of conscience from the very start. This does not involve more general values and norms yet, but very limited, concrete points, which are inherent in a situation, and are used as starting-points for direct action, based on an emotional relationship with an identification figure. This process is the first impetus towards the development of conscience, in normal infants too. Structopathic children have incipient conscience development, if there has been adequate socio-therapeutic approach for some time. A functioning develops, which, on the one hand, is a symptom of growth, but on the other hand is a sign of – temporary – danger. 'L'analyse contribue largement à fortifier ce moi encore si faible, et à favoriser son développement, en abaissant la pression excessive d'un surmoi beaucoup plus écrasant chez l'enfant que chez l'adulte', Melanie Klein (1959, p. 24) states with respect to the child, who even before treatment was suffering from a consuming super-ego because he is neurotic.

Rambert (1963, p. 28) also mentions these problems concerning neurotic children. 'Le surmoi de l'enfant serait effrayé si l'analyste accueillait avec joie ses explosions d'agressivité et c'est son moi qui serait effrayé s'il les condamnait'. The conscience of the child with severe behavior disorders, and specifically the structopathic child, will only start developing during and thanks to treatment. The danger of too rapid a development with respect to an ego which is not only childish but also disturbed, is very great. The therapist, gradually instilling emotion and structure into the child,

51

achieves calm and comfort with the latter, and an emotional relationship with the former.

Thus he becomes the identification figure. The child appreciates his real or imagined behavioral possibilities and establishes a norm because he wishes to be just like him. As indicated before: this is very concrete and inherent in the situation. A nine-year-old girl, under treatment for some months and showing rather more regulated behavior in the group compared with the school situation, made up her mind (as was only apparent afterwards; this incipient norm from within often remains mute) that, when she started school in the afternoon and would probably have to do her sums again, she would not throw away her exercise-book as before, or tear it to pieces and express herself in strong words, but finish the job.

This first independent step of a structopathic child is mostly bound to fail because the self-imposed demand is too exacting, or, to put it differently, the development of conscience is likely to require too quick a pace compared with the ego-weakness. This makes for a situation of stresses developing not only from without, but also from within, adding auto-frustrations to the already overwhelming frustrations.

Redl and Wineman give an outline of two types of insufficient frustration tolerance (Redl; Wineman, 1951). This intended as a distinction in behavior types. Experience shows that apart from this correct classification there is another, genetic possibility. Children of the sthenic subtype have the same reactions as regards frustration tolerance as asthenic children, when treatment first starts showing results. This indicates that a development of conscience is on its way. For auto-frustration, due to an inability to cope with the self-imposed norm may not only lead to direct aggressive reactions, but also to quieting down, bottling-up of emotions and repeated spasmodic efforts. After some time the tension can no longer be checked and will be released, often unexpectedly and seemingly inadequately. It will be clear that this whole process asks for thorough observation and a sociotherapeutically justified approach on the sociotherapist's part. Slowing down this partial development using relativity, 'Fremdschilderung' (Dührssen, 1960, p. 176) is a very useful technique. It may seem immoral, but in fact it is correct from a sociotherapeutic point of view, since one-sided growth threatens complete, and therefore real development, because it slows development down and may even lead to complete destruction.

4. PSYCHOPATHY OR SOCIOPATHY?

Quite often structopathic children are erroneously taken for neglected children. But they are also classified as psychopathic children.

We would be going too far at this stage if we entered into the problems of psychopathy. Suffice it to say that thorough investigation of children, diagnosed as being encephalopathic, endocrinopathic or neuropathic for want of a more appropriate term, may occasionally show that some of them are structopathic. Sociopathy is not so much taken as a separate syndrome in this connection, as described by Robins, but rather as a specific and clearly ascertainable trait, which can be found among some sthenic structopathic children. It is the phenomenon of 'gnawing at relationships'. Some children with apparent relationship disturbances have a way of being not only elusive themselves when entering a relationship, but also of ruining every developing or already realized bond among children and between children and adults. Techniques are used such as: direct aggression, incitement, intimidation, insinuation and nagging. Structopathic children with sociopathic traits as an accidental phenomenon are not on a level with sociopathic children. Their behavior is not only occasioned by disturbances from the milieu but it can also be traced back to contact disturbances caused by intramental defect functioning.

It would seem superfluous to discuss criminality when we are talking about children at kindergarten and primary school. There is one aspect, however, which needs further consideration. Experience shows that the likelihood of children from the sub-group discussed in this study becoming delinquents later on must be seriously taken into account. 'Professor and Mrs. Sheldon Glueck in the report of their recent survey of 500 delinquent boys found that over 50 percent of these boys had demonstrated symptoms of severe behavior disorder by the age of 8 and nearly 80 percent by the age of 11' (Rexford, 1956, p. 196). Also Clarke points out that children with a disturbed labile personality structure may go off the rails later on. 'In the absence of ample meaningful ways of assessing delinquent personalities, much attention has been focused on the external environment, and the basic personality has tended to be neglected. This is surprising, because it is obviously the interaction of specific personality patterns with certain life-experiences which goes to explain delinquent activity' (Clarke, p. 160).

Correct treatment, started in good time and attaining a certain degree of success contributes towards preventing criminality, apart from the positive moment of personality structure.

5. TOWARDS AN EMPIRICAL DEFINITION

In the first chapter we explained our approach to problem children. It was possible to classify them into sociotherapeutic treatment types. In chapter II we discussed the possibility of a formal classification, including the structopathic child as the first treatment type. We continued in the next chapters with a more detailed description.

Characteristics of structopathy

Summing up, we can formulate the following characteristics, point by point.

1. There are serious problems in up-bringing, which the milieu as a social situation does not explain and which occur wherever the child may be – family, neighborhood, relatives, school.
2. The behavior is characterized by great instability: shorter and less frequent spells of apparent calm, adjustment and infantile attachment alternate with protracted, more frequent and more intensely experienced spells of unrest. We can observe great instability, increased irritability, hardly any willingness to make contact, very volatile interest, failure to observe frequently and clearly stated social rules and demands. If the child encounters obstacles which in fact are small, the result now or later will be aggressiveness, sociopathic behavior, destructiveness or more vehement expressions of discomfort. Sometimes aggressive, pseudo-sadistic, sociopathic or destructive behavior occurs, which should not be considered as neurotic mechanisms or other milieu reactive behavior, but only pre-integrative and pure outbursts of passion (but see again chapter 3, section 1).
3. It appears from accurate observation that the child has primary and general learning difficulties. He does not suffer from complexes or problems, which would narrow him down in his perception and as an individual. His observing and perceiving existence, directed on the world, is very fluctuating and discontinuous, whether he is busy or not.
4. Psychological examination shows defective functioning, characterized by:
   – A disharmonic intelligence structure. The functions of visual analytic-structuring perception and motor-conceptual structuring are relatively weakly developed.
   – Attention pathology, characterized by a highly fluctuating attention span.
   – A poorly developed, poorly integrated personality with very diffuse

Gestalt-perception, great volatility, lack of concepts and content, and a social-emotional development which has barely got going.

5. In all the cases, the defective mental functioning could be traced back to neurological malfunctions, operative early in the genesis. They were mostly of a diffuse nature but were sometimes accompanied by cerebral defects, which could be localized.

6. An indirect fact is that the child can hardly analyse and structure the (social) situation, if at all. This is supported and confirmed by the results of psychological research.

7. Because of their inability to structure and receive structure, structo-pathic children have serious disturbances in their ego-development and should be classified having an ego-deficiency in this respect.

8. The development of social-emotional functions is severely retarded. Structopathic children can be characterized as pre-social and primitive-emotional. Their inability or very limited ability to enter a relationship seriously hinders the identification-process. Owing to this and to disturbed cognitive and social perception, they do not develop a conscience.

Empirical definition

Our definition of structopathic children, based on the preceding discussions and summaries, would be as follows. *Children characterized by typical and serious problems in up-bringing, which, as a rule, become acute during infancy, occur in all life situations and cannot be explained as milieu-reactive. These problems entail discontinuous and diffuse perception in their world owing to diffuse, neurologically defective functioning, preventing this perception from manifesting itself age-adequately in structures and from being structured by the individual, so that his genetical structuring does not take place or is severely retarded.*

This development disturbance affects all facets of the individual and the integration of the various function areas. Such children are charac-terized by a limited ability to learn, a lack of historicity, disturbed ego-development, pre-sociability and primitive emotionality, in due course attended by feelings of being threatened owing to their poor perception of the social surroundings. The normal social milieu and its resources appear to be insufficient.

This is apparent in the absence of identification and an incipient development of normativity, as well as in the malfunctions mentioned. Restiveness, alternating with drops in energy, increased irritability, reduced willingness to make contact, very fluctuating and oscillating

55

attention span, inability to observe simple and necessary social rules, direct or delayed aggression and discomfort are more peripheral behavior characteristics, which can be observed daily.

6. TREATMENT AND BEHAVIOR CHANGE

The structopathic child is characterized by a lack of structure. He is the exact opposite of the formalistic child, e.g. the autistic child. The structopathic child has no formal behavior patterns. If you visit our residential treatment center where only structopathic children are treated, you will, however, meet children who occasionally manifest slightly formalistic behavior, resulting from the phases in which the remedy is effected.

There are three phases in the overall treatment of structopathic children. In the first, treatment attempts to achieve an initial structure, a beginning of ego-development. In the second, the growth from within begins to develop, but still needs thorough guidance, especially as regards the social-emotional aspect. In the third phase, the child is confronted with the normal milieu, for example sending him to a normal school, and ensuring support, guidance and consolidation is provided at the residential center. This study deals with the first phase.

Most structopathic children, especially those of the asthenic subtype, tend to show slight formalising during the second phase of treatment. Not only their incipient conscience development (see this chapter, section 3) but also an awareness of their condition, which can be seen as growth, leads to a rather conscious, spasmodic covering of their disintegration. Nevertheless structopathy remains an underlying reality, and this defect manifests itself by severer stresses. Graphically speaking, the way to remedy, to the left of the continuum, is an undulating line, decreasing in width: lack of structure and formalistic behavior alternate. Treatment should be very tactful: using formalising as a means, but avoiding too great a habituation. As the picture outlined here only manifests itself in the second treatment phase, the misleading attendant formalistic traits cannot make initial diagnostics difficult.

Besides this formalising as a transitional phase (developing into normal behavior by way of line C–D; see chapter 2, section 2) another form of formalism should be pointed out. Among more than a hundred children, some proved to have a neurasthenic disposition apart from the neurologic damage they had received. The medical report mentioned in particular symptoms of vegetative lability. These children were found to show diabolical formalism on a primitive vital level, apart from clear struc-

56

topathy. Their treatment is seriously hindered because they exist in a vicious circle: disintegration will lead to severer vital spasmodic behavior, rapidly leading to an increase of tension, this in its turn leading up to the next explosion, and so on.

This concludes the description of the structopathic child. In the next chapters the strategies will be discussed.

5. Description of the treatment type: the strategies

1. INTRODUCTION

The disturbance type as a coherent multi-disciplinary picture implies a 'demand for treatment'. The answer is primarily given in the form of a 'first strategy'. This is a total treatment plan and serves as a general answer to the disturbance type. It applies to all individuals who can be included in this type.

The demand resulting from the structopathy disturbance type was formulated earlier on to stimulate continuity and structuring. So the first strategy will have to create specific living conditions, which can work as a therapeutic climate and as a potential treatment in all its aspects, and can give continuous structure as well. In a subsequent stage of treatment the individual must be given scope to develop, so that he can be adequately structured for his age and give structure to his relations with the world. Ideally, with increasing independence and responsibilities.

Now that the views on structure giving aid are rapidly becoming familiar, correct evaluations and misconceptions appear to be developing side by side. Giving structure has nothing to do with authoritative behavior or directive operating. It is neither training nor purely external moulding. Habituation in the favourable sense will clearly start playing a role, as in any up-bringing and as the result of any psychotherapeutic approach.

Giving structure aims at explicitly employing all that can be ascertained as a primarily spontaneous process in all development and up-bringing. It must be based on necessity, and aimed at stimulating development – i.e. expectant stimulation of growth from within –. The child finds himself in situations which are entirely or sufficiently realistic, and can be handled so as to remain clearly structured for this particular child, who is deficient on this particular point. So we are concerned with a methodical handling of situations.

The structopathic child does have severe disturbances: his chance of 'humanization' is limited. So he cannot be 'patched up'; he must have a professional and specialized approach for some time. This cannot be realized in the family situation, because the family may not be reduced to a treatment center. Since the children often come from good families, we need not discuss foster-parents.

Second-grade strategies which are embodied in this complex of first grade strategy, are employed as remedial agents. Of these, special education in a specific school is best-known and has received most attention. In the relevant literature it tended to be the only aspect to receive proper attention. Apart from function training, given in the special education, other forms are required as well. Motor therapy stands out in particular. In the cottage-group, methods are applied with respect to ingenuity and social behavior. A structuring approach aims to stimulate disturbed development in a clear and methodical way. The degree of the structopathic child's disturbance is so severe, however, that this alone will not do. If we are to proceed to treatment as described above, the children must first be given an extra push, to prepare them for treatment. This is achieved by structuring group therapy, which was specially developed and examined for the treatment of structopathic children.

The development, and particularly the testing of a complexity, such as a 'block' of strategies, can only be done step by step. So we had to make a choice. We started out by examining group therapy both clinically and experimentally over a period of six years.

For this reason we will briefly discuss the first grade strategy and most second grade strategies in this volume. Structuring group therapy will also receive full attention.

2. THE FIRST-GRADE STRATEGY

Residential treatment

Structopathy not merely causes disturbances in learning at school. First and foremost total personality development is endangered, so a specific climate must be created, in which adequate treatment is possible. This cannot be realized in the family. Attempts to achieve this by specific approach at school give insufficient insight into the problems. If the child has no other treatment and is allowed to stay at home, this is explained away with vague, sentimental and incorrect ideas on the ideal up-bringing situation at home. In reality, inadequate treatment counselling puts the parents off. And eventually the child will suffer. Residential treatment centers are a necessary evil, but it is essential for structopathic children to remain there for a while.

The views on residential treatment and therapeutic community are not new. Efforts to create therapeutic milieus and the desire to work with small groups were congruent at first. Corsini mentions Mesmer's (1776) approach making use of the suggestive effect of group sessions (Corsini, 1957, chapter 2). Pratt's efforts are well-known; he tried to cure tuberculosis patients with the aid of his 'class-method' early this century. Some decades later Marsh set forth the idea of a 'therapeutic community' and of 'milieu therapy', in which 'all the personnel of an institution would be involved in a common effort to develop themselves to the fullest extent' (Marsh, 1931 and 1933).

Especially when attention is given to the emotionally disturbed child, a shift can be noted from 'part-time psychotherapy as treatment and residential treatment center as a "depository"' to treatment in a socio-therapeutic institute equipped with supporting psychotherapy. Alt (1960, pp. 4–5), gives an instance of this in a psycho-analytic setting, outlining a number of features of residential living conditions as treatment possibilities and typifies the supporting role of psychotherapy with the question 'how psychotherapy needs accordingly to be modified so as to blend into a unified treatment approach' (pp. 135–136). We must not overlook Aichhorn, who was the founder of this idea. Fortunately none of these views suggest the situation described by Polsky (1963): that one pins all one's faith to one hour of individual psychotherapy, regardless of the negative influences of group processes which are operative as well. A more complete use of the possibilities of a therapeutic community is couched in Rapoport's view (1960); he wishes to create a therapeutic milieu, using the community as a remedial agent. Although the therapeutic milieu is not always explicitly mentioned, the same line of thought is followed by those who wish to apply social group work or group dynamic principles to the residential setting as such (Bennis, a.o., 1961; Cohen, 1967; Maier, 1961 and 1965).

Apart from Jones (1959 and 1968) and Gill (1967), we should also like to mention Llorens and Rubin (1967); they indicate a more detailed program and discuss the emotional and social aspects of behavior regulation and many aspects of function training (including a number of curriculum scales).

Redl and Wineman (1963 and 1967) express a different line of thought concerning residential care and therapeutic community. Instead of a sociotherapeutic treatment group, receiving partial psychotherapeutic aid, they create small groups and a continuous and thorough treatment plan. This is more of a group-therapeutic perpetuum than a cottage-group.

Financial consequences apart, we wonder whether the children might not have been confronted with an otherwise excellent and operationalized procedure, but in a too stringent and constant way. The phenomenon 'treatment-shock' might just as well be viewed from this angle. In Stone's work a similar procedure, though little elaborated, can be found (1966). He treats a heterogeneous group of disturbed children, in small communities of four, as if they were emotionally neglected. These include children with the hyperkinetic syndrome and severe ego-disturbances.

Cruickshank's views (1967) approach a therapeutic milieu for structopathic children: '.... the brain-injured child must be accepted at all times in terms of the meaning of the situation to him' (p. 149). Living conditions must, therefore, be clearly structured and structure-giving (p. 238).

Treatment in the cottage-group

This consists of round-the-clock treatment in a specific residential setting. This setting, its assistants and material equipment embody the 'structure-giving' approach. There is a therapeutic climate, in which understanding, acceptance and support become tangible. This first strategy, aiming at structuring in and by a more continuous existence, materializes most clearly in the cottage-group. The living community is handled as a group, thus enabling group methods to be realised as moments of treatment. This group work is utilized to approach the disturbed child not merely as a group member but also as an individual. It is a means rather than an end. Group living is of the utmost importance in the residential treatment. Here the child lives, and all other treatment aspects will only be really effective if they are directed on this center and are integrated into life. 'Group living constitutes the most unique feature of a residential care and treatment program. Therefore, group living can be visualized in the center in the formulation of a residential treatment program ....' (Maier, 1961, p. 132). The importance of the individual as group member is discussed by Cohen (1967); he states that being part of a group is essential to effect a 'change'.

How are we to treat structopathic children in the living community? We can only deal with this aspect briefly; we cannot claim that the following survey is complete.

We should like to point out, to avoid misunderstandings, that total treatment of the structopathic child takes two to three years. In this period three phases are distinguished. Treatment is different in each separate phase.

In the first phase we meet the structopathic child in his lack of structure. Especially during the first month of treatment the chaos this child consists of can be clearly observed in all its aspects. A newly formed living community of structopathic children is an incredibly incoherent collection of elements full of panic and arousal. They wander around without apparent reason. They fail to make contact, but do not fail to frustrate one another.

In this first period of the first phase, the group workers try to prevent all superfluous stimuli and arousal to habituate the children to their environment and to the fixed items of the schedule. This is not done for training purposes, but rather with a view to giving them their first foothold. Their 'leisure' hours are well planned and programmed with very simple activities which are as attractive as possible for the children. In so far as attempts are made to raise a particular concrete kind of behavior to a higher level, no more than one item is handled by all guides. Occasional periods of rest will gradually develop and the results of the structuring group therapy will make themselves felt.

In the course of the second month there is an increasing chance of treatment, which is effected on two levels: a level of more intensive treatment in small groups, and a level which is focused more on existence than on training. Starting with the latter: a great part of the leisure hours is spent on a well-programmed schedule and the child is expected to participate on the level which on the whole he can achieve. By giving structure to the situation, disintegration is prevented as much as possible. This (play)-programming seeks to create possibilities for prolonged 'infusion' of what was studied in specific training situations (second grade strategies, e.g. motor training). It is obvious that the recreative aspect also plays a very important role. The child feels at home with the group workers: he can vent his feelings of joy and misery.

More intensive treatment is carried out in small groups. At least two guides are continually present. During the longer spells of spare time, one of them works with a group of three to four children. The other guide works with the others, as described above. Within the small group, activities – games or expression for instance – are performed, lasting e.g. one hour, with the purpose of making the children function on a somewhat higher level, both cognitively and socially. This small group is a step farther than group therapy, because the peers and their activities have more scope for variation (which at first does not take place) and because the living area is subject to more arousal.

If the group workers use direct treatment by structuring the cottage-room – also materially –, by anticipating the presence of the child (e.g. when he comes back from school), by correct programming of their social intercourse and by a controlled and deliberately emotional process of becoming a person (which is far from simple), then the first structure will tend to develop in the child.

In the second phase, if pure structopathy has been mastered, and if the child has developed a certain degree of structure, slight formalising will mostly take place: a temporary neurotisation as a transitional phase to normality. It is as if the recovering child protects himself against relapsing into lack of structure by – somewhat rigidly – refusing to leave the beaten track: he is conservative and formal in adhering to what is familiar to him and withdraws when faced by new or complex situations, which are of course dangerous. On the one hand he will be allowed this formalism, as a 'natural' protection against renewed disintegration. On the other hand, we are intent on preventing him from getting permanently spasmodic.

In this period the child will have to be treated very tactfully. Treatment clearly becomes relativizing and liberating, allowing for an occasional somewhat spasmodic withdrawal. This cannot, however, be avoided. At first some children, who are in danger of disintegration, may still need a mildly structuring approach.

Finally, in the third phase the child begins to stand on his own feet. This also applies to the less protected milieus. For this reason he will start attending a normal school, which will help to make the definite transition both to his home and a less special school milieu less radical. He visits normal clubs, where he has to assert himself among children of his own age. He will have to mix with them of his own accord, because he is no longer considered to be disturbed. He goes home more frequently, and takes up his place again. He will have to experience home as the normal surroundings, not a vacation address. During this third phase, however, he still spends considerable time in the treatment center, which serves as a reception center for the child, who is now experimenting more independently; it also 'escorts' his activities out of doors. The child is particularly threatened by the rapidly developing conscience function; this imposes norms and may lead to a breakdown of structure. The child's self-imposed tasks may be too arduous for his developing ego. Failure to come up to the self-imposed norm leads to stress from within, which may be more disastrous than the stress from without used to be. In anticipation of the statistics in volume II, we can add the following. It appears that approximately 65% of the children offered for treatment could be helped completely within the fixed period. Some of the children who cannot be helped so satisfactorily become mentally defective during the latency period (± 10%), and some degenerate as a result of progressive suffering (approx. 3%). The rest of the children remain the objects of constant attention, study and research.

The therapeutic climate

The therapeutic climate is an aspect of the first grade strategy. It permeates all the living and treatment processes throughout the first strategy. The atmosphere and rhythm of living are the same: the child encounters and recognizes this in all individuals and events. Just as the first strategy varies according to treatment type, so will the therapeutic climate vary in keeping with the specific need for each separate treatment type. It is not therefore a matter of 'applying' the theories of one psychotherapeutic school, if this were indeed possible, because a therapeutic climate is not based on a second grade strategy. Nor is the therapeutic climate something vague like 'make love, not war', which would at the same time offer a fair chance of escape from the bitter necessity of treatment. If one wishes to find an analogy to a therapeutic climate, it cannot be derived from an individual therapeutic situation. The therapeutic climate is related to the normal situation of up-bringing.

Good up-bringing also implies a healthy climate in which children thrive. If the atmosphere and regularity break down, the milieu loses its formative value, its stimulation of growth and development. In both pathological and healthy situations a basal climate is necessary for development to become or remain healthy. This climate is prior to all technical and methodical action.

Although this does not account for the therapeutic climate as an existential relationship, two components can be distinguished. There is *atmosphere*, an emotional climate, in which understanding, acceptance, appreciation, tolerance and expectation are always basally present, in order to be actualized. They are such that their elusive presence can be sensed. The children's awareness that they really do 'belong' makes for thriving participation. This aspect may evoke anti-therapeutic ideas. Nevertheless difficulties in up-bringing are found among children who in a way lacked some '*living rhythm*', a certain degree of supporting regularity. For some types of children with severe behavior disorders a rhythm that can be easily grasped is essential during treatment. With others, with more pronounced emotional frustrations, a merely basal and directly

64

emotional approach proves to lead to chaos. It is not realistic therefore to blame the failure on those who execute this strategy. A severely disturbed child who never got a hold on our world might be more in need of regular security than normal children are.

As far as existential security is concerned, it cannot be offered occasionally, and especially not verbally, but should, as an underlying idea, be securely lodged in ever-recurrent things, in a certain degree of order, in a living rhythm.

The aspects of 'atmosphere' and 'rhythm' will be differently emphasized in every sociotherapeutic treatment type. As far as the former is concerned, the actual emotional climate needs to be different for structopathic and emotionally disturbed children, though the elements remain the same. We must develop a more 'scanned' rhythm and regularity for the structopathic child. The highly formalized neurotic child needs a more diffuse order than the normal child. The severely formalistic (e.g. autistiform) child, will have to be forced to break through the desire to persevere in fixed patterns, which no longer constitutes a healthy rhythm. The therapeutic climate is a – collective – existential relationship. Though material provisions are essential, the assistants are the ones who really 'form' or provide the therapeutic climate. They embody the 'therapy'. So it is most important that the group workers can function as fully therapeutic personalities, thanks to coaching and organisation, communication and participation.

As far as the structopathic child is concerned, the view that a rich, fairly emotional climate will necessarily lead to remedy should be rejected as incorrect and simplistic. If retarded emotional development is one of the results of primarily cognitive disturbances, treatment directed at providing the individual with scope for growth by means of a specific approach will also more indirectly affect emotional development. A much more structured therapeutic milieu can give the brain-injured child the support he needs (Cruickshank, p. 238). This has already been discussed by Bettelheim (1952). He speaks of insufficiently organized personalities. 'Love is not enough' to restore order to this chaos. It should be preceded by the experience of living in an ordered world. Compulsion is out of the question, the child is to realise that this ordered way of living is more agreeable (ibid. pp. 25–37).

The emotional climate as an intermental state is, therefore, used as an aspect of the first grade strategy during treatment. But it should fulfil a number of conditions. First, inherent emotionality can only be allowed to take shape in well-considered doses; it must be supplied in balanced quantities since an overdose will inevitably lead to chaos. Next, the emotional climate should be related to and integrated in the total treatment schedule, which is mainly aimed at supplying structure; so the climate should offer adequate chances of emotional structuring.

During the initial period of treatment, the right atmosphere, an adequate emotional climate, must provide stability and rest, preventing the children from being subjectively threatened. The result is that prolonged conditioning is unnecessary. An improved ability to analyse and structure all kinds of real-life situations also implies improved social-emotional perception and verbalisation, because they now approach totalities as such. The 'radar apparatus' becomes operative on an emotional frequency. The fact that they do not receive what is offered or only register it as arousal occurs less and less and eventually disappears. The normal sensitivity to emotion and emotional development gets going. A clearer understanding causes subjective and imaginary fears to disappear. Thus concomitant panic reactions become deconditioned. Later, when the first symptoms of normal emotional development are observed, the atmosphere will have to guarantee sufficient possibilities for realisation. Here again excess should be avoided.

Possible temporary formalising must be properly used as well. Children who have benefited from treatment to such an extent that they can master their emotions need not be considered since they are no longer structopathic.

The way back

Let us conclude our survey on residential treatment with the child's relationship with his own family. It is essential for him to feel he belongs somewhere; he belongs to his parents, he has his own place in the family because he is one of the children. He is part of a complex pattern of vertical, but more especially horizontal relations. Obviously the structopathic child who is still at home experiences this very vaguely or not at all. His social-emotional perception is also disturbed. The very placement in the treatment center evokes a vague awareness and experience of these relations. It is typical of structopathic children that at first they only experience placement positively. They rapidly feel comfortable and are not so keen on going back to their family in vacations and weekends. Back home, they would rather return to the center. The parents often find this very frustrating, although they have received information on this point, especially because the child expresses these feelings in a very concrete way: when he eats, goes to bed, plays with his friends. Sometimes, towards the end of the first year of placement, but mostly in the course of the second year, he is eager to go home again. He may start feeling home-sick too. Despite this experience genesis, it should be kept in mind that living conditions in the center are artificial; simply a means that enables him to go back to his own milieu. He is offered specific chances of growth on his parents' behalf and for their sake. This alone necessitates satisfactory co-operation with the parents, though there are other reasons too. The causes of structopathy are inherent in the child but come about within the family. A good family in particular attempts, consciously or unconsciously, to adapt themselves to the inadequate fulfilment of roles. They look for educative means and create situations which they think will help to stem pathology. This causes them to alter their own and their other children's roles. If the structopathic child leaves the family, he finds himself in a peculiar situation. The developing pattern of roles and mutual expectations can now be modified into more normal behavior and relations. The children at home will realise this sooner than the parents. But the parents as a rule need more relaxed relations as well. Many of them gradually lose sight of the necessity for brothers and sisters to keep the place of the absent child open. It is not so much concrete absence – the role stops functioning and atrophies – as relief once the disturbing factor has disappeared. If the parents become aware of this situation, they tend to make forced attempts to keep the place open. This may lead to a new spasmodic situation.

It is important for the structopathic child in the treatment center to be in his own family at regular intervals. This prevents the concrete tie from breaking for a longer time, to arouse his desire to go home and to meet this desire when it occurs later on. Besides, he must as it were be given the chance to practice more normal adapted behavior and to have a checkpoint to make sure whether the treatment is really effective, and not only mock-adaptation to the living community. He must have a chance to regain a more normal place among his brothers and sisters. The parents must become confident that the advised handling gives less tension but better results. Their 'change over' and the child's new role should be prepared well ahead of their definite return. This should be kept in mind right from the outset of placement.

Even if the structopathic child's family is normal, the center must regard it as a client-system because of the various reasons mentioned. It is up to the change-agent, already briefly referred to, to evaluate the frequency and the duration of family contacts. He should weigh up the desirability of continuity in the sociotherapeutic milieu on the one hand, and of short stays in the child's own family on the other. He must keep in touch with both parents to give them an idea of the child's situation, and remove unduly developed feelings of guilt. This in itself will be sufficient to relieve the strain.

Especially the short periods the child spends at home require planning in advance and consequent evaluation. One of the objects is to modify the parents' attitude implicitly, not only with regard to the child in question. Their relation with their other children must be such that these can grow up in a healthy climate, yet keep open the place of their structopathic sister or brother. The parents are inclined to expect guide-lines as to how to organize communication with their disturbed child and prevent difficulties. Experience shows that prolonged discussions about the child, going over a single behavior aspect and looking for the best – especially situational – preformed reactions to his behavior, are highly rewarding. If contact develops satisfactorily, it is not so much due to the technical content of the 'counselling' as to the calm and confidence which were the outcome of the interview with the parents.

3. BRIEF SURVEY OF SOME SECOND-GRADE STRATEGIES

We have stated that our choice makes limitation necessary. In this study we are mainly concentrating on structuring group therapy. The first grade strategy and the other second grade strategies are only dealt with summarily.

Motor therapy

Training of the motor functions of the structopathic child is vital supporting therapy. Since he suffers from the choreatiform syndrome, we have in mind a rhythm-motor training situation, preferably in small groups. This should regulate the coarser, but especially the finer motor system. Our chief aim is to improve the senso-motor substructure in so far as this is the basis of higher functioning. Next, we aim at facilitating improved and more integrated development of the higher cognitive functions, thanks to this improved substructure. Finally, this aids and aims at personality development as a whole, especially because the group situation is an additional factor in promoting social development. The last two, and more remote objectives clearly indicate the tie up with the first grade strategy.

'The school' is also an important second grade strategy. Education is not only needed for a return to the normal educative situation later on and for entry into society, but school normally also constitutes an important moment in the every-day life situation, because it takes up a considerable part of it. Besides, it may constitute a unique institution for the disturbed child. Besides a proper didactic approach, sociotherapy in a stricter sense may also be applied. A therapeutic climate (quasi-important educational matters can be passed over if necessary) can also be created.

For the structopathic child suffering from general learning difficulties and consequently disturbed in his learning at school, a residential school with a specific character is the obvious solution. If treatment is making progress, complete or partial use of a normal school could be considered, while placement in a center is continued. Thus the transition to a 'normal' milieu may be effected gradually. The necessity of a residential school results from the need to realise one continuous and structure-giving living milieu. Sociotherapeutically speaking, the school is an aspect of treatment. Next, the school must cope with the specific function-disturbances. Training of the motor and sensorial systems, analysing and structuring of time and space and auditory discrimination should be sufficiently co-ordinated with the more specialized separate basal training of the functions, and should take shape in and through education. This entails finding a proper balance between special training and what can be achieved by education in a stricter sense. Then we can really speak of special education.

4. FORMAL PLANNING OF THE STRUCTURING GROUP THERAPY

Structuring group therapy is one of the second grade strategies, but a very special one. Its function in the total treatment program is to make this fully possible. For that reason it was studied above all and examined both clinically and experimentally. Of all aspects of treatment, it will be discussed in detail.

Problems

Eight years ago, when the views mentioned so far began to take shape and when there was some possibility of creating a setting for treatment, real results proved, after some time of steady labor and evaluation, to be lacking. To our mind, the group workers were not to blame. These people had received good education, their work provided them with further training and they became specialized in this treatment type. They were enthusiastic about their work and research and achieved high-level methodical group work. Though the children made some progress in the sense of getting accustomed and adapted to the circumstances, their behavior did not change essentially. This was especially obvious in situations of slight stress and when these children were at home.

The group workers mainly attributed the problems with which they were daily confronted to the size of the groups (10 to 12 children). Management and staff appreciated this complaint, but took it at first to be a general wish to reduce groups. Little by little, however, they were to realise that one can only learn how to analyse and structure situations if these situations are not very complex. As complexity is not only based on the size of the group, but also on skilful handling of the situations, reduction of cottage groups to four or five children (which for that matter would not be feasible financially) would be a very simplistic solution. Besides, it would have the disadvantage of an 'over-condensed' continuous treatment, leading no doubt to shock-effects. So attempts like those by Redl, Wineman and Stone were set aside.

Purpose

Former experience with non-directive psychotherapeutic treatment of poorly-structured children did not only convince us of the incorrectness of this approach, but also of the idea that emotionality could neither be taken as cause nor as point of impact. Owing perhaps to this, the idea of some kind of group therapy did not develop earlier. The following solution was, however, the logical outcome of the considerations mentioned in the preceding paragraph: a small group under a guidance so expert that giving structure by therapeutic handling of situations is possible. Next, a restriction in time, due to the compactness of this approach.

The *purpose* was to enable the child to practice and to prepare himself to analyse and structure a real-life situation. This situation needs constant and inconspicuous handling, in such a way that it continues to give adequate structure. Thus, the child gradually develops the possibility of simple structuring and therefore, in addition, develops a primitive structure. The child has the pre-rational, and at first also pre-verbal, experience that he finds his life more agreeable and less disturbing in that situation. The result aimed at is not complete recovery, but a chance of further help in the sociotherapeutic cottage group, because the child,

70

now having developed a perceptive-cognitive capacity to a certain degree, can also analyse and structure the social-emotional field.

Working-method

Formally, the concrete working method can be described as follows. Within the existing cottage-groups sub-groups are formed, consisting of children who receive initial treatment and are therefore dependent on structuring group therapy. From the point of view of group psychotherapy and group-work in general, objections might be raised against the formation of groups out of only one cottage-group. But the choice is very limited, often preventing an ideal arrangement of therapy-groups. 'Clients' in special groups may profit by not associating with persons they already constantly meet in their living situation. The level of personality development and the purpose of the treatment decides whether structuring therapy groups are to be composed of children from the same cottage-group. We aim at a preliminary structuring, by which the child can lead a more meaningful existence in the living community and can be approached. Practice shows that the level of development is so primitive that all learning activities are very concrete. The transfer of the newly experienced behavior to the cottage-group situations is at first not only achieved in those kinds of play which were used in the therapy group, but also exclusively with those children they played with in the therapy group. Therefore sociograms in the first phase invariably determine the formation of sub-groups within the cottage-group. Little by little the new ways of behavior are also realized in other play or non-play situations and with other children. Structuring therapy has gained its end. Only now can socio-therapeutic treatment in cottage-group and school start. To achieve this a very intimate relationship with the child's own cottage-group is necessary.

The latter is not only effected by putting the children in the same cottage and therapy groups. A less condensed, congruent continuum is the continuation and basis of the compact 'practice' situation in therapy, which can be called a 'condensation of time': the atmosphere, possibilities and approach in the cottage-group. This can be achieved partly by training and coaching the group workers in this manner of treatment. Next, by discussing the child's behavior realizations during therapy-sessions. They are compared with his performance in the cottage-group. All this is not new. Guidance and supervision in this sense have often been described.

These forms of guidance may, however, have the disadvantage that sometimes no more than understanding and insight is the result, which does not guarantee appropriate handling. A method which has success consists in letting group workers watch therapy sessions by way of the one-way-screen. This direct experience, which at the same time means complete participation, including acting, feeling and understanding, is more rewarding than years of discussion. The workers participate in this concrete relationship, which allows them to transfer it to their own situation, without imitating the same intensity in practice. And so they will make fewer mistakes and become more confident. Kritzer and Philips (1966) mention analogous views, though not carried to this length.

This is one of the ways to make cottage-group and therapy-group a workable entity. It must, however, be noted that we cannot allow group workers to be present during therapy with the experimental groups; the whys and wherefores will be given later on. Practice has shown that the best relation between 'condensed' experience in the therapy group and the less-exacting but similarly structured living situation in the cottage-group is: for one hour, twice a week, at intervals of three to four days.

Since it is our purpose for this to be the first impetus to total treatment, the therapy period had to be short, especially the behavior therapies, not only to work more economically, but also 'to make psychotherapy more efficient' (Phillips; Wiener, 1966). This idea also finds favor in psycho-analytic circles. Malan (1967) gives a survey of former and current en-deavors and achievements. All these attempts can only be analogously used for the structuring group therapy, because they differ widely as to purpose and clients, since they sometimes aim at complete remedy of accidental symptoms. On the whole the patients, most of whom are adults, are slightly disturbed.

We learned that approximately 30 sessions were sufficient to give structopathic children an initial structure. 70% of them could get further treatment in the cottage-group. This means a therapy period of fifteen weeks, which is practically equivalent to the first four to five months of the treatment, taking into account a one to two week assimilation period directly after admission and intervening vacations. Of these 70% there were some, specifically intelligent, children belonging to the asthenic sub-type, who displayed slight neurotic superstructure even at the end of this first period of treatment. This required a somewhat non-directive, therapeutic guidance. Other asthenics were found to develop this later. The remaining 30% included some children, specifically those belonging to the chaotic sub-type, who showed no results. Others proved to need continuation of the structuring group therapy. When they were in a sufficiently advanced state, they were able to thrive and grow in the cottage-group. This might mean continuation of this treatment in another therapy group if their own group were dissolved.

72

One might wonder why this supporting therapy is performed in particular as group therapy. Would individual approach to the child with severe behavior disorders not be better? Is he already fit for the group with all its attendant social problems, such as competition, sharing things and a code of its own?

In the literature concerning small groups as a medium of treatment, both in social group work (Wilson; Ryland, 1949; Kaiser, 1954 and Konopka, 1963 give useful surveys) and in group therapy (Corsini, 1957), the idea generally prevails that the group gives the individual chances of becoming socially experienced. These social experiences should be evaluated both positively and emotionally. Scheidlinger (1954) also indicates as one of the objects, the reorganisation of adapted patterns.

Our ideas on the main object of group therapy have been strongly influenced by, on the one hand, our having to do with (slightly) emotionally disturbed children, and on the other hand by the fact that emotionality has been overstressed as the cause of disturbances. People who deal with severely emotionally neglected children state that they must first recover and grow by means of individual contact with an adult therapist. Hart de Ruyter is one of the few who fully accepts the consequences of this: he refuses to leave the child to the group when there are no therapy hours, because the child is not yet fit for it.

The specific problems of the structopathic child lead to another matter. Development of analytic perception and structuring action in real-life situations is the main object. Social and emotional development are indirectly involved, but they are not the point of impact. The real-life situation in the small group with patients of the same age is very suitable because it can give structure. 'New behaviors are practiced *where* they are needed (in the group) and *when* they are needed' (Miles, 1961, p. 725). Modification of the perception of the social world is only possible when an in-group is created (Lewin; Grabbe, 1961, pp. 506 and 508).

A more accidental but nevertheless very real fact, suggesting that treatment should be primarily effected within the group, is the experience that structopathic children are quick to lose their temporarily poor form when establishing direct, individual contact with an adult. Any group worker will experience this abnormal increase of physical and mental hyperactivity if he addresses the child directly, either praising or controlling him. Those who in their capacity as motor therapists, speech-therapists (and other specialised professions) normally apply individual treatment, comment that it is difficult to realise this with structopathic children, far

73

more difficult than in group approach. We are of the opinion that, when establishing individual contact with the disturbed child, the emotional aspect in the manner of approach – involuntarily and uncontrolled – has a greater impact than in more indirect contact, within and by way of the group, which is by its nature more matter of fact. Where individual contact is necessary – take for instance the life-space-interview (Redl, 1966, pp. 35–67) – the adult is expected to exhibit a great extent of self-control, if the interview is to be effective and not doomed to fail because the child starts showing a lack of structure.

Therapist's role

The theory 'group approach rather than individual' raises some new questions. What is the role of the adult, i.e. the therapist within that group? It is a striking contradiction that we might wish to treat children as group members, even though they are still ignorant of a social world because their perception and cognition are disturbed. Then surely the therapist is compelled to occupy himself with individuals simultaneously! In other words: are we not dealing with a number of vertical relations, whereas horizontal relations are lacking?

First and foremost, the structopathic child is in himself a contradiction: as a human being he depends for his 'humanization' on spontaneous growth developing in his relation with others, whereas he lacks the normal possibilities to establish it. The problems broached in the preceding paragraphs are therefore not merely a theoretical fad concerning the advantage of group therapy compared with individual therapy. We are concerned with the essential disturbance of the child and his treatment. Purely individual contact does not appear to yield situations which are essential for treatment and at the same time have a destructuring effect. The group forms the surroundings where the first break-through towards education and growth can be achieved, but horizontal relations are practically absent and the danger of individualizing vertical contact is imminent. How is the therapist to play his part?

A simplistic, logical solution would be to avoid vertical contact. In that case the child would depend on horizontal contacts, when he is in need of relations. He does not, however, feel that need. Vertical contact would not develop, but clashes would interrupt a solitary existence, whether active or not. A passive 'wait-and-see' attitude on the therapist's behalf turns into a 'laissez-faire' attitude. In order to prevent total destruction and accidents it would be advisable to take immediate action. If not, the child will not be brought up or have positive support. He will experience threatening interruptions of his activity, leading to feelings of strong discomfort. Thus therapy turns the most ideal situations into further structopathizing.

It is the therapist's task to handle, with a minimum of individual relationships, the situation in such a way that horizontal relations develop. His part in these relations should be minimal and planned, clearly structured, and programmed play themes should achieve horizontal relations in the first place. The child, engaged in his play, should be unaware of this. The object is to train analyzing perception and give structure in the child's actions in positively experienced real-life situations. In this way contact with children may remain indirect and somewhat matter of fact. Here again there is an antithesis. On the one hand, the therapist's personality behind this methodical operating generally guarantees the success of the treatment. He should not be a shadowy figure, but one of flesh-and-blood. His individuality must enable him to participate in the situation and offer himself to others (Stoller, 1968). On the other hand, he should, in his relation to the structopathic child, be more 'role' than person, as is evident from what we have already said. He tactically avoids too much individual contact and realizes the situations by means of a particular, constantly adapted role-performance, so that the children can remain situationally involved in what happens, and more or less achieve role realisation.

There is a clear difference with non-directive group play therapy for children with behavior difficulties. We know from experience that the difficulty with both kinds of treatment does not lie in the children's 'difficult' behavior. The therapist's efforts in the non-directive approach result from his having to look out for problem manifestations which the child expresses both in play and conversation. This does not enter the first phase of treatment for the structopathic child. The major difficulty in carrying out structuring group therapy is handling the 'personal-non-personal' approach, which requires a great deal of practice and constant attention, because naturally one is apt to offer oneself to the disturbed child spontaneously.

In structuring group therapy, the therapist achieves the situation by stimulating the children's roles through his role-performance. The structure should be sufficiently plain for them to keep in touch. Whenever the situation looks like being no longer sufficiently structured, either because it becomes too difficult or too varied unexpectedly, or because drops in energy or frustrations inhibit the ability to structure, the therapist must provide a solution in time by means of his role-realization, which calls for great ingenuity. At first this stimulation and direction of play in advance will take place so soon before the child's role-performance and seem so much like a demonstration that what the child does is in fact imitation. This demonstrates clearly that the child *learns* how to play and *learns* how to give a situation a structuring approach. It is a well-known fact that during training of normal adults by playing a role, imitation likewise plays a more important part than improvisation. Bandura's investigations concerning the significance of model and imitation are self-evident. As the child starts developing, the therapist will be able to play opposite him instead of structuring the play in advance, because the child is more capable of prolonged self-realization; 'doing things together' becomes 'playing together'. After the first half of the therapy period the therapist can withdraw from the activities for some time, but he takes a part which enables him to return to the play situation at any time.

A single instance may suffice to elucidate what has been said above. During play, a child visits a shop and buys a cake. The play-object in question is so beautiful, besides being the only item in the shop, that the child who plays the part of the sales-girl is reluctant to part with it. Now the situation and children alike lose their structure. While the child is in the process of refusing, the therapist enters the shop, as a baker, salesman or the like, trying to deliver cakes. While the signal leading to destructure is welling up in the child who refuses (often inferred from his mimicry) or is penetrating the peripheral part of the other child's nervous system, at any rate before sub-cortical panic and discomfort break loose, the therapist restructures the situation. He neither orders nor forbids them, he does not impose limitations, neither does he entreat, beseech or cajole. The therapist does not leave the creative atmosphere, but gives structure by way of role-realisation, which entails a role-expectation at a certain distance.

In non-directive therapy it would have been possible to delay varying intervention, in order to give the children a chance of committing themselves, to let them experience the emotional reaction of others or to solve a problem. The therapist might also have entered the situation and used the problem for reflection either directly or later on by means of play situations or verbalisation. In so far as is necessary, he can use his personal-emotional relation with the child in order to teach him how to handle frustrations. All this cannot be realized with the structopathic child, because he is not yet fit for reflection and must be protected against disintegration. His 'ability to learn' is still very limited. He should first function under protection on a low level, before he is fit for reflexive behavior later in the treatment. The above example concerned children who are already fairly advanced. They have already realised some creative play on their own. Earlier in treatment, notably with the younger child, the therapist will have to look for solutions to effect a gradual transition from playing a role in advance to stimulating structure of a group happening. In the sixth chapter we will elaborate on what actually happens in therapy groups.

As the child makes progress in and through the therapy, a shift occurs in the therapist's self-realisation. The developing ability to structure a situation appears to bring about inner structure, so that the child will not only be able to 'understand' and tolerate his companions better, but the therapist will also be able to approach him as an 'emotional' individual, without the child having chaotic reactions. A process has taken place, analogous to one described by Bennis and Shepard regarding dependence and interdependence (1961): 'The evolution from phase I to phase II represents not only a change in emphasis from power to affection, but also from role to personality ..... This development presents an interesting paradox. For the group in phase I emerged out of a heterogeneous collectivity of individuals; the individual in phase II emerged out of the group' (p. 339). One might also wonder whether initially role-regulating behavior does not have harmful conformity pressures on the children's individuality and creativity. In a more general sense Cartwright and Lippitt observe: 'Strong groups do exert strong influence on members toward conformity. These conformity pressures, however, may be directed toward uniformity of thinking and behavior, or they may foster heterogeneity. Acceptance of these conformity pressures, towards uniformity or heterogeneity, may satisfy the emotional needs of some members and frustrate others. Similarly, it may support the potential creativity of some members and inhibit that of others' (p. 276). With the structopathic child, individual personality and creativity are not in danger of being levelled off by the 'strong group', the structuring therapy group, during the initial stage of treatment, because neither exists. We aim at basal arousal of both. In the next part of this chapter and in chapter 6 we shall reveal how, after stimulating this foundation as the initial form, the treatment accompanies individual development by means of creativity.

Play therapy

Structuring group therapy is carried out as play therapy in a play room. This will not be surprising, considering the age of the children treated and especially their level of development, which is highly infantile, also in nine and ten-year-olds. Nevertheless questions have arisen in practice, when specially-trained psychotherapists or students became familiar with structuring group therapy, either by observation or participation. During the first sessions many differing behavior aspects are noted compared with neurotic children. For instance: lack of rapid positive or negative relation formation, little ability to make contact, chaotic behavior when approached in a normal emotional way, inability for creative play, and hyperactivity leading to no creation at all. Notably therapists in training who have had some direct experience with more established forms of play therapy or have created (magical) ideas about psychotherapy from literature, are apt to become frustrated by their first therapeutic contacts with structopathic children. Failure of the session is an easily discernable but not very deep-seated cause. It would seem to us that actual frustration results rather from a lack of satisfaction because the 'therapist' does not feel that the experience was productive. Is, therefore, the play-room eminently suitable? Would it not be better for these children to play ball out of doors? The rules of the game are sure to give structure. The choice of the play-room is related to several factors. The same play-room must be used every session because of the children's concrete requirements.

The number of stimuli should be limited, though they need not be entirely lacking, as for severely mentally disturbed patients. Structopathic children are more labile than the labile reaction type differentiated by McClure (1964) in play groups, and also have a weak ego. Because of their lability they are subject to stimuli which are either too strong or too numerous. The sthenic sub-type can moreover, according to Haufmann's classification (1963), be included in the destructor type. Regular destruction of the available material does not have a structuring effect. Various forms of outdoor play, mainly requiring much, directed mobility and some understanding, enable some types of disturbed children 'to let off steam' in a healthy way. Redl and Wineman indicate how outdoor play can also be applied with aggressive boys in order to use previous satisfaction images as resource (1951, p. 115).

In the case of structopathic children this type of play primarily stimulates hyperactivity. It is not long before the child runs the risk of losing his co-ordination and conscious intentionality. For this reason, such play should be restricted and cautiously handled during the first phase of treatment in the cottage-group. As all activities, it should take place under strict guidance. This kind of play will not do as a therapeutic situation. Not only because it might result in destructuring, but also because there are no possibilities to stimulate and train, by way of varying situations, the creative mental powers for structuring and planning of present and anticipated circumstances. That is why regulated round games and painting are less suitable for the concentrated learning situation in the therapy. It is quite possible, however, to use them in the cottage-group. Finger-painting and sand-and-water play are completely out of the question because of their strongly liberating nature.

Experience shows that for structopathic children too, creative play (see Haworth, 1964) is an eminently suited therapeutic means. Its application should be clearly distinguished from that of other treatment types. The play patterns are neither employed to expose complexes, nor to assimilate them during play nor to integrate new healthy ways. The structopathic child is incapable of creative play. This is not due to inhibited functioning, as may occur with neurotic children, but to a lack of this function. At first, play situations are realized with great difficulty. Careful planning is of vital importance. Planning cannot, however, last any longer than one to two minutes. It is mainly a matter of imitation; there is hardly any ingenuity or variation. Constant support is needed, flexible and energetic aspects are absent. Everything that takes place during the first sessions savors of a learning situation, although the children do not experience it as such. They experience these sessions very positively. They have some experience of a pleasant, regulated and planned existence. This 'learning how to play' stimulates and develops creative functioning. The purpose goes beyond the sheer ability of creative play. Normally a child can achieve this kind of play because his ability to structure in the present is shifted to the future. Group play therapy develops structuring and creative foresight by means of play. The structopathic child 'learns' from these data how to order the present, how to preserve some relation to the immediate past and how to anticipate and realize what the next item will be. Continuity develops and becomes more and more extensive and intensive. Later on it also starts functioning in other situations. At first, handling of creative play material is difficult for the structopathic child. This applies especially to puppets, the use of which requires flexibility in changing roles. The children play a part, which they really try to be. The data on role play mentioned in several studies (Kelly, 1955; Levit and Jennings, 1961; Corsini, 1966) are not very useful for structuring group therapy, considering the enormous difference in level, development and possibilities between the developed, slightly disturbed adult and the structopathic child. Interesting, however, is Kelly's 'prescribed role therapy'. The client has a concept for his role, which he is expected to read through three times a day. The direct planning and constant structuring of the situation in the structuring group therapy strikes us as being analogous, the enormous shortening of the distance accounting for the difference.

Since the essential aspects of the therapy will be extensively discussed in the sixth chapter, we shall not particularize them further at this stage.

The structuring process

Since the type of group therapy described constitutes one coherent action, we have inevitably mentioned structuring, giving a short outline of how this process, by dealing with situations and the therapist's own role. Similarly, we have already enumerated in reverse order the gradation in structure-giving levels: the possibility of still treating the children within the creative atmosphere, the need to leave the creative atmosphere, setting limits to the situation as well as to the child, command or prohibition. Clearly one always aims at the highest possible level, though lower levels may have to be entered, but only if clarity for the child necessitates it.

Is the structuring nature of the initial treatment of structopathic children so exceptional that it makes this therapy completely different from other therapies? For it might be suggested that structuring is used in the group therapy of structopathic children but not in the other therapies. We do not agree, however. True, during treatment of less severely disturbed children the child must be given the initiative to a certain extent, while the therapist preferably has an understanding, wait-and-see attitude. But no less a person than Allen points out the danger that the therapist might hinder the therapy by showing too much kindness and understanding. If one does not set limits, one assumes that the child with behavior difficulties will be able to do so himself, unlike non-disturbed children of his age, who are unable to do so (Allen, 1942, chapter 8). Help in finding the limits in play and personal situations is discussed by practically all child psychotherapists and they consider it a problem quite often. The development of limits in love-relationships is described by Crocket (1966) as a general and con-tinuous process in human social development. In all child psychotherapy, more structure is given by the implicit processes when the child is placed in a therapeutic situation than by this external structure-giving process, when borderline situations are reached. Bales demonstrates that the initiation of behavior items by evoking reactive behavior and relation patterns is committed to certain structural patterns (1951, p. 468).

The idea that disturbed children – individuals who are being brought up – should be treated by offering structured situations, is gaining ground. Haring and Phillips reject a non-directive climate for the emotionally-disturbed child because they feel it is unstructured; they are in favor of clearly structured situations. But a climate, in our view, is only unstructured if the non-directive element is overstressed and is realised without being adapted to the child. They intensify this structuring character by analysing what they are doing in that situation in limited, conveniently arranged 'elements' (Haring; Phillips, 1962, pp. 9–12).

Structuring does not, therefore, make group therapy for structopathic children altogether different from other therapies. The distinction rests in more explicit handling. Also when we do not give direct structuring but the situation is handled to that effect, this is not done as a matter of course, but consciously and systematically, since it is inherent in the sociotherapeutic situations. We do not aim at letting new structures grow spontaneously through a liberating approach, but prefer to let the children experience and approach for the first time real situations as structured ones, thanks to a more directive handling of the milieu. The explicit, conscious and systematic use of structuring as principal means to give structure, clearly refers to the *directive* nature which structuring group therapy can assume, especially during the first sessions.

A clear distinction should be made between a directive and an authoritative attitude, as described by White and Lippitt (1960). The 'directive-non-directive' tension field, where education and therapy operate, is different from the 'authoritative-democratic' field and does not run parallel to it. Directive behavior is possible without any trace of authoritative behavior.

If the course of any treatment whatsoever is expressed by a line, it will be a curve, undulating between the directive and non-directive poles. This 'wave' line may be wide or narrow. In the latter case it may be nearer to one of the poles. As a rule, the curve representing structuring group therapy will run obliquely: at first close to the directive pole, then through the middle to the non-directive side.

We use the terms directive, suggestive and affirmative and speak of a suggestive approach if the child is capable of achieving a structuring process without receiving a directive but rather an indirect approach, so that he himself thinks that he is in control of the action. When we ask: 'Now John, why not try to be a real shopkeeper' this is extra-creative, directive structuring. 'I think that John would make a good shopkeeper', is in fact equally directive but allows a bit more scope for individual activity and creativity by presenting it to him differently. This can be termed suggestive. This is a clear case of 'le ton qui fait la musique'. We use the term 'affirmative' when the child is allowed to take the lead himself in the prestructured situation and when his behavior is stimulated and continued by affirmation. We think this term is more correct than the non-sociotherapeutic and therefore unrealistic term 'non-directive'.

Programming

The play situation can, to a large extent, be structured by programming. We suggest that this aspect of providing structure clearly distinguishes group therapy from other kinds of therapy. In group therapy for adults with poor personality development Solomon, among others, programs the group happening by giving a 'message' to the group members (Solomon;

Berzon; Weedman; 1968). For children, especially structopathic children, it is too arduous a job to keep this up and carry it out adequately during the complex happening which the play group with its constantly alternating situations is. Programming will have to be more extensive, concrete and repetitive.

This also requires a feed-back possibility. Regular checks are needed to see whether the program has really been understood and can be transformed into acting. When this is not or only partly possible, supplementary concretization should be given with a minimum of disturbing interruptions.

In connection with investigations concerning the modification of communicative behavior, with young children as well, Flavell (1968) states: 'These observations suggest what may have been a basic inadequacy in the training programs used: insufficient control over the educational inputs to the child. In these two programs E did little more than put children into a situation in which they *might* obtain formative experiences, that is, experiences which could give them new insights into the nature of the communication problem. He did not, however, keep careful track of whether any given child actually *did* obtain such experiences, and above all, almost never intervened in order to make *sure* he did' (p. 206). During the structuring group therapy sessions the 'program', the play schedule, was never left to chance. It was always arranged in advance by the group members and the therapist. The children's contribution depended on the extent in which they showed initiative which could be carried out in practice, while taking into account each other's ideas, interests and plans. The independence, ingenuity and social feeling which are necessary for this, mostly fail to function in structopathic children until the last ten to fifteen sessions of the therapy period, depending on the growth that has meanwhile taken place. This, in its turn, is related to the degree of structopathy and intelligence, and, to a lesser extent, to age.

We can therefore distinguish levels in programming. At first, planning is necessary outside, but very close to the playroom. In the playroom the stimulus of 'beginning' is too strong. For this reason it is not only impossible to stimulate the concentration needed for the interview, but above all, a non-programmed start leads to hyperactivity and chaos. On the other hand, planning slightly removed in time and space from the playroom, will obliterate the traces of the discussed plan, because of the short distance which has to be bridged. The interview begins by inquiring about the children's plans. At the end of the preceding game and between times they have been invited to 'think' about it, preferably together. After the children have been attuned to one another the therapist starts substantiating the wishes uttered by planning them in time and space, while the children themselves give more and more support. The building up of the play situation with the aid of play material is a highly concrete repetition. The children must repeat essential points several times verbally. The 'performance' will at first only last a short time (a couple of minutes), because they lack imagination and because they are not capable of a further development of variations and verbalisation. As a rule the children ask for a repetition afterwards. Strong support is necessary to give more substance. A differentiation in subsequent program items is a means of simplifying programming even more. The first item is performed, followed by a short intermission to remind them of the next item and to repeat it briefly, etc. At times we use this method with children who are so severely structopathic that they cannot play together along structured lines in any other way. No matter how high or low the level, the therapist will always have to check the role-play and, if necessary, provide the feed-back needed with his own performance, or with creative or real information.

The increase of possibilities reduces the therapist's analysing support in this respect too. Planning, which can be started in the playroom, and realization are transferred more and more to the children, until they reach the level on which the therapist is only necessary as a catalyst. Meanwhile, Corsini's 'behind-the-back-technique' (1957) can be applied, where possible and necessary, to consider programming and results. This is done in an adapted way, to be dealt with in the sixth chapter, in which the more conceptual aspects of programming will also be treated.

Summary

The purpose and method of structuring can be defined as follows. The structopathic child suffers from an inability to move in his world in an adapted way, due primarily to cognitive disturbances. In all situations aid will have to be focused on offering the child realistic possibilities to function positively in this respect. This is done very consciously and explicitly in structuring group therapy, on the one hand by concrete and directed programming, on the other by the therapist's continuous support, mainly in creating discernable situations and in fulfilling a particular role. At first both the creative and realistic approaches will be of a more directive nature, making way for a 'suggestive' approach, followed by a more 'affirmative' type, related to the child's capacity to analyse simple play situations, and give structure to them, which will enable him to receive structure himself.

We can summarize by defining structuring group therapy as *an intensified sociotherapeutic procedure, closely related to and serving the cottage-group situation, in order to offer structopathic children optimal chances of an analysing and structuring approach to real-life situations, by means of adequately handled and programmed – mainly creative – group play situations in a playroom, so that they themselves receive an initial structure, thanks to positive experience of living in a structured and more continuous world, which enables them to profit from sociotherapeutic relationships and treatment in the cottage and school group.*

The therapist's task in this formation process shifts from more directive role-realisation and substitutional structured and structuring ego, to a more affirmative capacity of entering a personal relationship.

6. The course of structuring group therapy

1. INTRODUCTION

Because we have tried to give a clear definition of the problems concerning the 'why and how' of structuring group therapy, and to facilitate the definition to start with, we have illustrated various aspects of this method and the therapist's role in the preceding chapter, organizationally and formally. Now we should like to discuss some important moments of this therapy in more concrete and conceptual terms.

In order to describe what happens as completely as possible, we shall deal successively with some salient features of the first, second and third phases, and we show the significant behavior changes the therapy will effect. The length of each sub-phase cannot be ascertained accurately. In this respect marked differences can be observed in each group. If we start from the groups which could be dissolved after thirty sessions, the average subdivision is roughly as follows: first phase six to eight sessions, second phase fourteen to eighteen, last phase four to eight sessions.

The rate of progress and the quality of behavior in general might show differences between older (8 to 10 years) and younger (5 to 7 years) children. We did observe differences in their varying interest in play and play material, which differed in the older children from boys to girls. As for quality and level, there were slight differences or none at all. The degree of structopathy and notably the quality of intelligence were ascertained to affect the extent of progress decisively. There were some older children who were clearly handicapped because they were late in receiving treatment: deconditioning took up a lot of extra time.

For six years over a hundred children were helped by means of the structuring group therapy. During the first three years, research was of a clinical nature. After that this treatment was experimentally tested for three years (See volume II for a description of this experiment and its results). It involved treating 15 groups with 53 children (see appendix I).

In this chapter observation data will be taken from experimental groups. Instead of random borrowing from all groups we only plan to handle the records of three groups, namely, a group of girls (BK2), a group of boys (MK3) and a mixed group of infants (RD1). This makes for more clarity and continuity in the description of the course of behavior during the three therapy phases mentioned. The children of the three groups will invariably be referred to as C1, C2, C3 and C4. These children will be described in appendix II.

One might also wonder to what extent the results of these three groups are representative of the whole. Volume II will discuss the fact that of the children treated 43.4% showed good results, 33.96% reasonable results, whereas 22.64% failed after thirty sessions. The three groups had the following figures: good, 54.55%; reasonable, 27.27%; no success at all, 18.18%.

These results are somewhat more favorable than the total average, mainly due to the absence of children of the chaotic subtype.

2. THE FIRST PHASE

During the first phase the structopathic child amply exhibits his inability and lack of structure. His chaos, as it were, makes him a prey to his world, at whose mercy he is. Inward or outward disturbances may cause his euphoric state of hyperactivity to turn either into actions or reactions of discomfort or into spasmodic calming down and withdrawal as delayed release, which sooner or later is expressed in no longer integrated motor and/or verbal 'deflation'. Because playfulness is lacking in this phase, play treatment strongly resembles a learning or practice situation because of the strongly explicit programming and the therapist's constant, intense support. His function is one of directing, organizing or suggesting from one moment to the next, creating clear-cut and comprehensible situations.

Programming

In chapter 5 we mentioned the necessity and significance of programming as an aspect of structuring. Likewise we mentioned the manner and place in which the 'plan' is discussed, viz. close to, but not within the playroom.

(BK2, session 3). Play planning next door to the playroom is not making much headway. When the girls are asked whether they have talked it over C 2 says that she wants to play doctors. She makes for the door to the playroom, because to her mind the affair is settled. When the others are questioned about their ideas C 3 chuckles and says that she is willing to join C2. C 4 is smiling somewhat absent-mindedly. Then C 1 says she is more in favor of playing 'mothers and fathers', immediately incurring an aggressive torrent of words, including excretions and a rather unpleasant sketch of her personality from C 2, rounded off by some venomous remarks on the part of C 3. C 4 is very attentive now and looks scared. The therapist claims that making a plan together is always the best policy and that it is quite common for a father or a mother to take a child to the doctor. Then C 2 is asked what the others are to play if she is the doctor. (The possibility that another girl would choose or be given this role is not touched upon to prevent the weak structuring from being overtaxed). She hesitates when giving an answer, becomes a little angry and says that they should make up their own minds and when the therapist remains silent she repeats the therapist's suggestion: 'mother and children'. C 3 excitedly remarks that C 1 might as well play the patient and that it would be a lot of fun to chop her up. C 4 remarks that a doctor is often accompanied by a nurse. The planning proceeds with difficulty. With the role of doctor in mind, substantiated by telling what kind of things he does, the other roles get some meaning and shape as well. Note that all this is almost entirely the therapist's doing. A short repetition of what was discussed only partly succeeds because of impatience and inability. Programming proceeds in the playroom with a concrete division of the space available and helping the children to plan the house, waiting-room and office (note: after 8 min. they had finished playing).

(MK3, session 3). The group went rather 'off the rails' during the busride (these boys were on their way from a treatment center to the university) and it takes some time before planning can be started. C 2 is in a very excited state, glowers at C 4 and tries to catch him. The latter is scared and dashes through the room, cursing and shouting. It takes some time to calm them down because, on the one hand, the process of destructuring has already proceeded so far and, on the other hand, the therapist does not know how it all happened. At first C 1 thwarts the therapist's attempts because he keeps making irritating remarks about C 2 from the background in a low voice, so that the latter flies off the handle again. C 3 keeps completely out of this and apparently has some difficulty in calling to mind where he is and why. After wandering around a bit, during which he touches everything, he takes a seat in the therapist's office-chair, saying cheerfully: 'In Mr. K.'s room ....; we're going to play again!... Shall we start, sir?' And suiting the action to the word he makes for the door. When the others have cooled down a bit the therapist can consent. After some difficulties the group reaches the room next to the playroom. Real group play cannot be planned yet. With a great deal of support the individual plans are structured to some extent: C 1 wants to be a garage-keeper, C 2 would like to play with Red Indians in the sand-box, C 3 is going to build a fortress with soldiers but doesn't want to have anything to do with the Red Indians, which is mutual. C 4 is at a loss what to do. Nobody sees any possibility of joining him. The therapist suggests that he plays with the train. Then there might be a slight chance of drawing the individual players together after all.

(RD1, session 3). Because nothing was achieved during the last play-time, the therapist suggests 'mothers and fathers', offering it as a story first. (This was what they wanted to play again). She tries to make the children fill in the story as much as possible; C 3 fails to do so, C 1 and C 2 are hardly successful. This story is then explained in successive elements which can be comprised in short sentences, each one serving as a program item. Only the first item is discussed in full and repeated, the other items are to be dealt with when the play reaches that point. In order to avoid complications, role-changing is not suggested as yet. C 1 is again father, C 2 mother, C 3 remains child and the therapist will play the aunt.

The above examples will show that programming during the initial phase not only takes place before but also during play. In these and subsequent sub-phases observation shows the way the therapist acts. For the most part it can be labeled programming.

What is most striking about play during this phase is the paucity of creativity and the inability to handle the course of the game: a failure to see the successive stages and the way they should be planned and an inability to retain what happened before. The latter should be the basis of subsequent actions and give direction to them. These children could be described as 'pre-creative' and 'pre-temporal'. In so far as they do not lapse into disintegration, paired with feelings of discomfort, they tend to exhibit a purely functioning attitude. When a child is pre-creative it means first of all that he is not or hardly able to play a role. Understanding of another child's role is a particularly difficult process.

(MK 3, session 5). Therapist: 'Look, now the thief (C 2) is going to hide in his lair'. C 2 responds to this suggestion and disappears behind the puppet theater with the goods stolen from the camp. C 3 jumps up and wants to go after him. The therapist slows him down. 'Yes, but C 2 has taken our blocks'. The therapist whispers that it is night and that the campers are sleeping. The thief, who must therefore not be viewed as C 2, has been so cautious that we, C 1, C 3 and therapist haven't noticed a thing. We won't wake up until dawn and we'll find out that nuggets (instead of blocks) have been stolen. Then we're going to tell a policeman (C 4) and hunt down the thief together with him. C 4, who has been fumbling with a toy wakes up in his police-station, puts on his cap, makes for the puppet theater, saying: 'Well, well, come along. You're the thief'. This activity is stopped and the thread of the story is taken up again, after the superintendent, with an aggrieved expression, has taken his seat behind his desk. With difficulty they wait for dawn (half a minute), discover the theft and find the thief's haunt after they have tracked him down with the help of the police.

It will be clear from this that the child can only see and handle his own role, but has difficulty with the others'; it is also impossible for him to keep at a distance from the direct and concrete facts, which are essential for creative play. It is precisely this possibility which, in real-life situations as well, guarantees his first growth. This keeping at a distance implies of course inserting a moment of reflection between the stimulus and the reaction to it.

The foregoing may include a temporal aspect, but defective functioning in this case (the fact that the child is still pre-temporal), is even more clearly illustrated by the child's inability to develop a plan for the future and to build on what had been achieved before. A mild form of this is a continuous meandering from the point, so that the connection with the original plan will soon be lost. Because this process of 'side-tracking' seems to happen step by step, we might get the impression that it is a rather continuous course. As such it might be compared to the play activities of infants, whose attention also tends to stray. First of all, this *might* be true of infants, but they certainly can stick to the point, especially when they receive some support. Moreover, structopathic children, as a rule, can no longer be included among infants because of their calendar age. More important, however, is that sudden divergences, or rather complete changes of subject, are too abrupt to be called 'meanderings'. All this is more apparent in the more serious form, which, as a rule, occurs more frequently, and in which the play elements are so detached that the 'divisions' are clearly apparent; these can justifiably be called fragments of 'now'.

(BK2, session 4). Finally (after the situation has been programmed and built up), play gets going. The doctor (C 3) is going to visit the wards and addresses the headnurse (C 2) who, arms akimbo, inspects the sick children (dolls) as though reviewing the troops. The ward-nurse (C 4) reports for the second time saying that a mother (C 1) with a child who is seriously ill is sitting in the waiting-room; the therapist stimulated her to do so. She's ignored by the doctor and the head-nurse. The doctor sighs and looks at the therapist with an enquiring look. The therapist speaks in a loud voice and assumes that the doctor is sure to tell the head-nurse that she's willing to examine the children. This happens and the doctor starts undressing a doll.
   In the meantime the therapist continues his story, but still without trying to establish direct contact: 'the head-nurse says that the nurse usually undresses the children for the examination and that she herself assists when it's a busy day. Then the doctor says which children she wants to see and gets her instruments ready'. While waiting for this to start, the therapist contacts C 1, who has left the waiting-room and the sick child and has started to play with the puppets of the puppet theater. The therapist proposes that she knock on the door of the ward in order to say that her child is seriously ill. The whole situation has suddenly changed. C 2 and C 3 have both set out to undress the dolls, after which they put on other clothes, fetch a pram and walk about with it. This is functioning, not another game. When the therapist stops the playing and inquires what's being played, the connection with the hospital situation appears to have been severed. In the course of the new planning (the therapist tries to make the children tell what's going to happen themselves), C 3 proposes that she becomes a shop-assistant. When asked about the connection with the game they were playing, everybody is silent, after which C 2 proposes to be a customer. C 4 attempts to establish a relation by proposing to buy some food for the children.

(MK3, session 6). It's not possible to carry out the simple plan, which is chiefly a repetition of the final result of the previous session. The few minutes of play accomplished thanks to strong stimulation and support fall away all of a sudden, to be followed by functioning or chatter, which cannot be explained by what preceded.

Apart from the absence of the temporal relation between the play elements, both as basis of what preceded and as guiding line of what is to follow, the short 'performance' is also striking. A bright spot is the third session of group BK2: play is achieved for eight and a half minutes after strong programming both before and during the play. Most sessions in the initial periods tend to be shorter, varying from one to four or five minutes, interrupted by spells of distraction.

If the group happening does not lead to discomfort, acting-out or aggression, their inability to play causes the children to lapse into a functioning handling of things. In that case they will mostly keep to themselves. Since sensopathic play rapidly leads to complete disintegration it was avoided. Sensomotor play is realised by letting the children play with toy-cars and puppets, by continuously repeating activities from an originally aesthetic game, etc. These activities do not usually last long either and lead to strong impulses to run about, to yell, to jump etc., and especially to clashes between children; the latter caused mostly by the sthenic type.

Frustration and aggression

We have referred briefly to the very low frustration-tolerance and the manifestations of rapid aggression several times, especially in the sthenic sub-type. This is the most conspicuous feature of their immediately perceptible behavior. The various ways in which they expressed this sort of aggression often led to placement in a center. In the first phase the cottage-group resembles a mine-field and the first therapy sessions result in many explosions. On the first scale of the rating-scale system, to be discussed and included as an appendix in volume II, most scores will be found on points 1 or 3; these indicate serious forms of aggression, like acting out or reacting.

The degree of aggressive behavior – obtained by means of observation – in the separate phases of therapy constitutes a fairly clear criterion for distinguishing the three sub-types. We shall discuss how the statistics reveal a significant difference on this point and justify a more specific answer in chapter 2 of volume II. During the first phase sthenic structo-pathic children are very aggressive. The asthenic control themselves better, are insecure and only occasionally exhibit delayed explosions. This is not necessarily bound up with what happens during the therapy-hour, because frustration pent-up during therapy may also explode outside these hours. Children belonging to the chaotic sub-type cannot actually be said to be really aggressive because they do not behave intentionally. This is more a matter of having 'reverberations' colored by comfort or discomfort, of which discomfort prevails; sometimes with aggressive undertones.

A striking aspect of this aggressive behavior in the first phase of treatment is not only the occasional acting-out, or any other lack of a direct connection with what actually happens, but also the fact that this aggression operates, so to speak, separately from other behavior aspects, such as a lack of self-confidence, of independence, concentration, team-spirit, ingenuity, contact with the therapist. Some connection seems, however, to exist with the degree of vitality; longer spells of activity and excitement correlate with more vehement and frequent aggressiveness. The stresses are caused by the inability to accomplish, by pure bursts of temper and by the behavior of the other group members. As far as the latter is concerned, this clearly need not as such cause stress at all. Disturbed perception and arousal project threats and result in frustration. It is related to the inability to accomplish play: this is also based on the disturbance mentioned. So we see that both self-control and 'realisation' of the situation get low scores in the first phase (See appendix on rating-scale system in volume II).

(MK3, session 4). N.B. This session was hindered by C2's frequently aggressive behavior. He started interrupting when the play plan was being made. Whenever any suggestions were made or his role was discussed, he tried to attack C 1 or C 4. During the game he was not co-operative and did not even get as far as individual function play. Quite often he disturbed the aesthetic or creative play activities of the other children, by pinching them or knocking over play things, by punching, calling names and throwing or kicking a big ball right through the playroom.

An outburst from C 3 could not be prevented. A fight was hard to avoid. After this C 2 threatened to leave. Because the therapist did not react and at the same time prevented the others from showing that it would be great if he went, he left it at that. Finally the therapist succeeded in making him collide his toy-cars, using pleasant, indirect suggestive stimulation: the therapist had been demonstrating for him for some time, while at the same time guiding the play of the others. Little by little C 2 came nearer and finally took over the game.

(RD1, session 4). This afternoon C 2 all of a sudden behaved very aggressively without any apparent reason. While he was playing with the train he suddenly got up, snatched away C 1's bear and flung it across the room. He rushed at C 3, kicked him, and responded to my interruption by punching, biting and kicking. I kept him near me and tried to soothe him. This made him relax, then he sat down for a while and began playing again. Later on he was unable to say whether he had been mad about something.

(BK2, session 5). C 1 was about to play the role assigned to her whilst the game agreed upon seemed to be getting going, and she did not want to play a role C 2 wanted her to play. This instantly aroused C 2's anger and she attacked C 1. The fight was stopped with difficulty. The children could be prevented from starting again, but the situation remained tense. At regular intervals C 2 let loose a torrent of abuse towards C 1, partly of her own, partly stirred up by C 3 and by the irritating behavior of C 1, who somewhat foolishly seemed to revel in provoking aggressive behavior. After her outburst C 2 was very quiet, pale and withdrawn. On leaving she suddenly flared up at the fact that it took a long time to get her coat on. Her behavior was so striking that the other children looked up in surprise.

(MK3, session 2). C 1 and C 3, no longer taking part in the game, were on their knees, looking at the puppets which were in a drawer of the closet. They were having a nice chat. Suddenly C 3 got up and kicked C 1's thigh with all his might. Nothing had been said or done which could have caused it.

From solitary functioning to play group

Gradual group play is another problem in this first phase. Although solitary functioning cannot entirely be prevented during the first sessions, we try to find ways to introduce group play from the outset.

(BK2, session 2). All the children want to play 'mother', and they dislike the idea of the four of them forming a family; it is beyond them. In the playroom the four of them are persuaded to go to a specific corner, which is their home. The material needed is distributed under strict guidance in order to prevent difficulties later on. They take up their positions and each is busy with a domestic job. Direct contacts are refused but they constantly watch and imitate one another. Before long, most of them appear to lapse into messing around. The therapist calls on C 1. He is an old friend who happens to be in town and who wants to have a gossip and a cup of coffee. The dilemma whether it is convenient for this very suggestible child is avoided because the situation baffles her. The visit is very pleasant because of the therapist's creative play, and he stimulates at the same time C 1's role. The others are fascinated but unwilling to co-operate. The proposal made to C 1 to go along and visit another friend is accepted. So C 1 and the therapist call on C 4 a minute later, who receives them enthusiastically. When they have played for some time the therapist proposes starting anew, but now all together. C 3 withdraws. C 2 refuses at first but is finally persuaded. This results in strictly directed play, lasting about 4 minutes.

Apart from the combination of individual quasi-roles, which is possible because they are identical, the preparation for group play can also be effected by material.

(MK3, session 3). (For programming see above). In a corner of the playroom C 1 is building a garage, partly hidden from view by the puppet theater. In the other corner, along the same wall, C 3 is building a fortress for soldiers. He is completely absorbed, does not want to be disturbed in any way and growls like a dog if others have a look at him or speak to him. C 2 decides he does not want to use the sand-box after all and builds his Indian camp on the ground. He quickly loses his temper when things go too slowly and he constantly needs the therapist's help and advice. C 4 has been jumping about, talking about building a railroad but has only succeeded in rousing the anger of the others, because his jumping about makes the puppets topple over and the fortresses shake to their foundations. The therapist gets him going and induces him to construct the rails so that there are three termini, near the garage, the fortress and the camp. Construction of the rails demands much support, because he has difficulty in fitting the pieces together and because he has no sense of direction. Half-way this work is delayed because C 2 thinks it better to build his camp in the middle of the room. So he not only comes in the area of the railroad, but because he is constantly crawling round his camp he occasionally upsets the rails, which shift and get damaged. Twice C 4 repairs the damage, grumbling and sulking, but when it happens for the third time, he starts howling, which especially frightens and irritates C 3, who is completely absorbed in staring at his fortress. Peace is restored and the therapist depicts the reality of the situation for C 2 and C 4, because now the railroad track runs through wild Indian territory. Mountains (blocks) are placed along the track, limiting and protecting it at the same time. Because especially C 2 and C 3 tend to lapse into functioning and boredom, a discussion is inserted, which C 1 reluctantly joins. The therapist tells a thrilling story about a train which is to take gold from the village to the fortress, but is attacked on the way by the Indians. The driver manages to reach a house, where a garagekeeper lives, and together they warn the captain of the soldiers who sends his men to investigate the matter. Gradually the game gets going; it can be carried out for some minutes. Constant support and intervention are needed, because, for want of creativity, a situation cannot be played coherently and because they cannot wait for the moment to play their own roles. (Even before the train leaves, C 3 has already stood his soldiers near the Indians; when, a little later the attack is imminent he rushes forward in advance, without soldiers).

If in this way group play gets going to a certain extent, point by point planning is often necessary at first and the children should be reminded of it. This has already been discussed and illustrated in the third observation of this chapter.

Impulse towards repetition

Finally, a typical aspect of the first phase, is the impulse for the children to repeat what they did during a former session. It will be a positive experience if the therapist, after a number of sessions, succeeds in achieving group play for a short time. Frequently, it can only be done at the end of the play hour, because of the time needed to plan, build up, prevent and solve conflicts and 'soft-soap' the children. A favorable point is that the play hour has a pleasant ending. Because a short, but continuous and pleasant experience is involved – perhaps for the first time –: 'play was great', 'it was a lot of fun', 'it's a pity time is up', a certain impression is made, especially on this vital level of satisfaction. Some days later when the next game is planned this vital recollection makes the children long to 'play the same again', which should be interpreted as 'being and playing together in that way, without interruptions, quarrels and disintegration', since these cause discomfort.

The children do not retain the content and structure of the game. This might suggest that we might just as well play another game, provided experience is the same. On the contrary: there is a vague vital recollection. The child wants to imagine it more vividly, and this can only be achieved if structure and content are traced back in fragments. He expects to learn this from the therapist. This can be labeled paucity, a quest for that with which he is somehow acquainted. We think it better to recognize in it the child's enormous concreteness. He looks for what is familiar to him, not on the basis of fear of something new, but to support and practice his both reproductively and creatively deficient imaginative faculty.

Little by little it will become possible to introduce extending variations. Completely new content is desired if practice has been effective. Then the child still appears to be so concrete that he can, to a certain degree, only imaginatively recollect and plan what has been played repeatedly. When asked for a new idea, his answers are vague. They often consist of fragments from a story or a TV series. The child is unable to make a fairly coherent plan, in spite of what he observed. Only after he has had a repetitive experience of some games will the functions of analysing perception, recollection and creation show some development. By then treatment has reached the second phase.

3. THE SECOND PHASE

Interested spectators who watched a play hour in the first therapy phase are most impressed by the aggressive behavior hindering the group activities and making the group difficult to handle. The foregoing will have indicated that the essential problem is more deep-rooted. Structopathic children must not be concluded to be children with severe behavior disorders because of their 'troublesome' behavior, but because of the many tricks in a specific situation necessary to start their function development and further up-bringing.

During the second therapy phase, the first poor results can be observed. The following descriptions are mainly derived from the middle and the end of this second phase because changes are not manifest until then.

Programming

Programming, both before and during the play, is still necessary, because only within and from fixed schemes is reasonably continuous completion possible. Substantiation during planning and play is, however, increasingly achieved by the children themselves. The discussions prior to the play can also be held in the playroom. It is typical that the children should desire, even demand, the therapist to join in, preferably in a leading role, although they accept that he mostly refuses to do so. The content of a game will occasionally be so satisfactory that the therapist might leave the children alone for some minutes and limit himself to suggestions and confirmations. The children do not accept this because they are still too concrete to be able to dispense with their concrete scheme, which the therapist embodies.

94

(BK2, session 12). This time the children quickly come to an agreement as to the content of the game, the roles and how these will be distributed. At the end of the last plan it was agreed that C 2 would be allowed to make a plan. The advice to talk it over in advance with the others so that much time for play would remain has been followed to a certain extent: shortly before going to the building where therapy takes place he had a talk with C 3 and C 4. C 2 tells the therapist that the game is 'about a school .... and a child that's punished .... and a mother who will go to the schoolteacher ....' after which an outburst of laughter makes further verbalisation impossible. When they have stopped laughing they enumerate some random content aspects. After this the therapist has to give a great deal of help to put things right.

(RD1, session 11). The children are keen on playing mother, father and child. They already have an idea who will to play whom and with some stimulation they also mention several content aspects: 'daddy also goes to his work .... he works on the railroad .... mommy starts making the food on the cooker .... the child is still young and may play at home and help mother sometimes .... but the therapist must be the maid; she knows what to do in the house and in the kitchen'. Gradually the contents can be arranged and enlarged upon.

(MK3, session 15). C 1 and C 2 have made a plan; C 2 scrambles through the main points. C 1 is more specific in his elaboration, whereas C 2 watches in an opinionated and serious fashion: he nods vehemently in agreement every time he recognizes items of the story. It will be a game about 2 robbers (C 2 and C 3), who are going to steal the Indians' horses. C 1 will be an Indian, if the therapist will be one too. A minor problem crops up; C 3 wants to play with the therapist. After some discussions, during which he is encouraged and the pleasant sides of his role are stressed, he accepts. The therapist asks the group what role has been assigned to C 4. C 1 says that C 4 refused every role during the discussion. From the outset C 4 has withdrawn to a corner of the room. He looks very gloomy and seems to be highly frustrated. No one knows the cause and C 4 himself cannot give a reason either. When C 2 states that play is to start and wants to suit the action to the word, C 4 starts to call him names and is on the verge of weeping. An outburst of temper from C 3 as a reaction to this is hard to prevent. After C 4 has been calmed down a bit by the therapist, he answers, when asked whether he wants to be a robber or an Indian, that he wants to be neither. From the intonation willingness to play is vaguely apparent. Soldier, superintendent, hunter etc. will not do either. Finally he tells what he really wants: C 4 would have liked to be the doctor. The therapist says that this is a great idea, who else was to tend the wounded? If he is a vet as well, he will not lack customers. The whole group feels relieved and this new element makes it possible for the boys to substantiate the plan. Now they can wait with starting right away, 'because without a plan the game will soon be over; and that's no good' (C 1). Their understanding of the coherence between the play elements, notably in a temporal perspective, is still pretty limited.

Growing independence: from directive to permissive

The games in the second phase are increasingly characterized by rather independent play. Rather, because a lot of support is still necessary and duration of the play remains limited, varying from fifteen to twenty-five minutes. Nevertheless independence is increasing, this is apparent from the change of support: the directive approach makes way for slight suggestions and confirmation. When this growing independence in achieving creative play manifests itself, we can speak of ingenuity and creativity. As far as the treatment of structopathy is concerned, it means the development of the ability to understand and handle situations both through perception and action. The child exhibits a better and longer attention span and though rigidity and fluctuation do still occur to too great an extent, apart from dips, such as drops in consciousness or energy, there is a distinct increase in continuity. When improved perception and cognition (which also serve as control equipment when the actions depend on a concept) are supported by better concentration, and when both creativity and memory pictures evolve, resulting in future planning, the development of historicity can be said to be on its way (see chapter 3).

The success of the games planned and the attendant feelings of comfort, tinged with some pride, give the children more self-esteem than any encouragement could achieve and result in an increasing degree of self-confidence; and not only an increase, but a change in quality. The sthenic structopathic child may occasionally give the superficial spectator the impression that he is not lacking in self-confidence. Self-assertive and tyrannic behavior, shouting the others down, undaunted approach to situations appear on second thoughts to be nothing but a strong impulsiveness not integrated and regulated in and by a superstructure, and a lack of real perception and insight. A kind of self-confidence is developing now, which can be characterized as openness and surrender. The latter in its turn underlies their ability to display a sense of team spirit.

All the aspects of personality development can be seen to grow very gradually. As yet they are very fragile and can be rapidly flooded by renewed disintegration. Not only stresses from the milieu are dangerous in this respect; therapeutic situations may occasionally show the phenomenon of too rapid a development of conscience (see chapter 4). Play realisation is the best means for the child to keep his budding personality development in check. Stresses that could arise from handling the situation are more readily anticipated and solved by better functioning, although failure in this respect will clearly occur regularly, but to a more limited extent. The ego, still poorly developed, cannot give sufficient resistance to stresses caused by others or by self-imposed norms, because the child is also subject to discomfort and consequential frustrations. Briefly: the child is getting a hold on situations, but the hold on himself is clearly insufficient. This is noted on scales 9B and 9A respectively (see volume II).

Involvement in learning how to handle situations is manifest from the curious phenomenon of the impulse to repeat. Contrary to their behavior during the first phase, when the children wish to repeat in the next session the pleasant experience of the preceding one, which they remember vaguely because of their poor development, the phenomenon is different now. During the second phase the children do indeed sometimes want to repeat a game they played during another session, not necessarily the session immediately preceding. The desire to repeat a game during the same session occurs more frequently. The planned game is now played more creatively, but the children cannot fill up the play period with it, nor can they perfect their 'performance' sufficiently. They are left with a slight feeling of discomfort when they suddenly realize that the game is over. During this phase they express the wish more and more to do it once again, but then better and right away. This manner of reacting, which takes the place of their former disintegration into discomfort, can be regarded as growth. On the other hand, their desire to repeat, because they are unable to exchange roles or to vary the situation, does point to their being still very concrete.

Change in aggressive behavior

A typical feature during the second phase of structuring group therapy is the change in aggressive behavior. Structopathic children of the *sthenic sub-type* not only behave aggressively less frequently, but differently too, at what we might call a higher level. Aggressive behavior as acting-out clearly occurs less frequently, and even disappears almost completely with most children. Next, aggression finds more verbal ways of expression and physical violence does not take place. The frequency and degree of aggression were at first proportional to pathological cheerfulness and vitality, but now a connection appears to exist between team-spirit and self-control. Other behavioral aspects also show that budding sociality constitutes the link between pure biology and expression. Their contact with the therapist also illustrates an increase in social involvement.

(BK2, session 12). C 3 and C 4 come home from school and tell mother (C 2) what happened there. The schoolteacher (C 1) was in one of her moods again and scolded and punished them. C 3 does the talking, while C 4 plays the whimpering child. C 2 patiently listens till the story is finished and urges the children to reflect whether this is the whole truth! She cannot be expected to go to the schoolteacher with lies. (This is C 2's own contribution to the story, during planning they had not talked about it). C 3 is baffled for a little while but then she starts telling the story again and emphasizes the details a bit more. C 2 stops the torrent of words, tells the children to be good and stay in the room and to touch nothing. Then she takes her bag and heads for school like a ship in full sail, after a detour through the playroom. C 1 has been listening and makes herself ready to counter the attack. When C 2 has rung the bell and has been shown in, C 1 is laughing somewhat nervously. When C 2 does not say a thing but only frowns at her, C 1 starts fidgeting, apparently she has some difficulty in keeping up her role and says that in her opinion the lady is wearing a funny scarf. C 2's expression turns gloomy and an outburst is possible. The therapist is just about to retrieve the situation in his capacity of headmaster. C 2 watches the therapist and with a sigh she starts asking C 1 whether it is true that her children have been treated unkindly. It is very striking that C 2 could digest this frustration and maintain her role, because during former games she quickly became irritated, especially by C 1. C 1 continues having difficulty in playing her role well and after the fourth or fifth time C 2 flares up rather aggressively: she says that C 1 is a 'childish bitch' and turns to the therapist to complain about C 1's bad performance and her silliness.

During the second phase the structopathic child of the *asthenic sub-type* exhibits a different change: his behavior clearly becomes more aggressive. Because he is growing accustomed to the play situation and his self-confidence is increasing, he no longer swallows frustrations till the safety-valve breaks down; now he reacts more directly to stresses. And because sthenic children, even though their behavior improves, naturally tend to cause stresses to the asthenic children, who are quickly threatened in this respect, aggressive behavior is rather frequent.

The preceding observation shows for instance that C1 was apt to display aggressive behavior and even used physical violence in this phase, C 4 from the same group also tended to puzzle the therapist and the two sthenic children because she no longer maintained her seeming frustration tolerance. This also involves change in the relationship with the therapist. It is not so much a matter of a decrease in contact, even though this does take place to some extent, but rather the very childish protection-seeking dependence (more in the sense of being 'committed to' than of being 'attached to') is observed to make way for somewhat more independent behavior.

(RD1, session 13). During today's play, we were struck several times by C 3's aggressive behavior towards C 2; formerly he would withdraw and isolate himself. C 2 was some-what put off his balance, but did not react with counter-aggression. Apparently he was at a loss how to deal with C 3's unexpected abilities.

(MK3, session 16). After C 4 had lodged at the police-station some complaints with the superintendent (C 2) that his car had been badly repaired – he suspects foul play – the policeman (C 3) is ordered to check the story by questioning the garage keeper (C 1). Once he is at the garage, C 3 does not succeed in playing his role properly. He is not creative enough to perform well. C 1 acts his part well; three times he asks him pleasantly what it's all about, but he barely gets any response. Suddenly he flares up and acts very aggressively. After initial surprise at his courage, C 2 and C 4 express so much admiration and approval of what he did that they tell the baffled C 3 that he ought to have performed better. All he can do is stammer, saying that he had forgotten the details.

98

Developing reflection •

A final remark: in the course of the second phase games some admiration is occasionally heard which is the *beginning of reflection*. Comments on the degree of success of a game or part of it are more frequent now and are no longer on the level of expressions of comfort or discomfort, but rather testify to a more realistic insight. The children still think it hard to analyse their shortcomings in play realisation well and to verbalise them. They have an inkling that they have made a mistake somewhere and mostly only blame the child who is supposed to have made the mistake, not as one who is playing a role but as a person. Nevertheless these reproaches are mostly not formulated until after the game and they are not couched in such gross terms as they formerly were.

(BK2, session 14). While clearing away things C 4 asks C 2 whether she liked the game. The latter says she did, but she thinks that when it was not nice this was due to C 3, who was messing things up. C 4 is of the same opinion and says that C 3 (her twin sister) can be a darn nuisance. If she keeps behaving like that, she might as well clear out.

4. THE THIRD AND LAST PHASE

Continuity

During the last phase of structuring group therapy its – limited – purpose is achieved: apart from relapses, the children prove able to lead a more continuous existence *in this situation*. They can obtain such a perceptive analysis of the therapy situation and of the varying play situations inherent in it that these become sufficiently clear to them and consequently no longer cause arousal or threat. Subsequent play realisation implies, thanks also to adequate manipulation and verbal reactions, that a concept can be executed. The functioning of both reproductive and creative imagination is bound up with this. They in fact constitute the continuity and make responding and initiating play participation possible. As we have said before, all this is true of these concrete situations. Though their impact becomes manifest in all other real-life situations (also at home) the children's performance is then decidedly at a lower level. This kind of group therapy, however, aims at making the child ready for further socio-therapeutic treatment: the last phase inaugurates the first phase of the total treatment, viz., the work already started in cottage group and school becomes effective now, in other words conceptual.

99

Programming   •

The level of programming before the beginning of a game continues to rise both quantitatively and qualitatively. The time needed is considerably shorter and intensity is higher; not only are their suggestions richer in content, but the children are also more successful in structuring these contents. The therapist's support no longer dominates their structuring. But support remains necessary, sometimes for the distribution and relations of roles, but mostly for the overall plan and final completion of the game.

(RD1, session 27). Today C 1 was allowed to suggest a plan. On entering the playroom the children take a seat round the table. C 1 explains what is going to be played. She will be the mother, C 3 the father (the latter laughs somewhat timidly but agrees, which implies that he does not want to be a child any more) and C 2 will be the man who works on the train. First, father and mother start packing the cases and dressing the children whilst C 2 gets the train ready. The therapist asks where they are going. C 1 hesitates for a moment. C 2 says: surely they can go to grandma. Right away C 1 takes over again. She thinks that the therapist should be grandma. Then they will call on her. The therapist agrees and asks what the man from the train is supposed to do during this call. C 3 thinks it rather simple: drive on. C 1 understands the problems better: he'd better call on grandma as well. C 2 is in favor of it: 'Then I would be your uncle' he says.

Higher behavioral level and integration

The children can now cope more fully themselves, not only with programming before play, but also with conceptual handling of it during the play situation; they can also manage and carry out unanticipated variations and extensions. The therapist's attitude, which of necessity must be a response to the child's behavioral level, is now mainly of an affirmative, or occasionally of a suggestive nature. The latter may be necessary because of the complexity of the game at some stage, but also to give preventive support to their individual roles. Good, pleasant games still tend to alternate with shorter or longer periods during the sessions when support is required, notably when the children have to get over their frustrations.

During this last phase their behavior is not merely characterized by a higher level of the various behavioral aspects, and at the same time a decrease in pathological 'cheerfulness' and 'vitality', but specifically by their harmonization and integration. For this reason the aspects described in the sections on the first and second phases can no longer be treated separately, without violating the behavior description or repeating ourselves. There is a close connection between reasonably independent realisation, control on the situation and themselves, and their diminished subjection to aggression consisting of acting-out or inadequate reactions.

100

This hold on themselves, which has not been manifest until now, can be considered to be the 'coping-stone', i.e. the concluding and formative moment of the beginning of a structured existence.

Hence it is a stepping-stone to a developing personality: this centralizing interiorisation is the beginning of an ego-genesis.

In the relation with the therapist the changes which were making themselves felt towards the end of the second phase become acute. We have mentioned the ability to give better affirmative support. This partly results from the more essential fact that the therapist can now establish a primarily personal relationship. Both changes are due mainly to the children's growth. Their improved ability to be independent causes a third change: the therapist can withdraw more and more from the game. During the first phase he was continually asked to initiate, continue and manipulate, and during the second phase expected to join in, preferably in a leading role. Now he can withdraw regularly and function as a catalyst. He must, however, remain aware of the necessity to assume a role if clarity of the situation requires it. Sometimes the children ask him to join in if there is a surplus of roles. To a considerable extent, however, the group can do without him. During one of the sessions, one of the group members, who did not show much progress, involved the therapist in the game. The other three did not accept that and managed to do without him, without eliminating him altogether.

(MK3, session 28). While C 4 (the medicine-man of the gang) examines C 2, and C 1 (the leader) withdraws into his cave to contrive new plans, C 3 (also a robber) goes to the therapist asking him whether he is willing to help him execute his task. Since the others do not object, the therapist agrees. When the toolbag, which was lost during the retreat, has been found and has been handed over to the leader, the new member of the gang (therapist) is ordered to go outside the cave so that the others can discuss whether he can be trusted. C 3 is to stay with him to keep a close watch over him. The three of them whisper; now and again some chuckling can be heard. Then the leader gives his orders: the doctor is to go back home, C 2 and C 3 are to go on a secret mission and the 'tenderfoot' (therapist) must watch the cave, into which C 1 withdraws to reflect. Soon afterwards C 1 asks the therapist for help. The latter enters the cave (meanwhile C 1 has left it) and looks for C 1 who is in distress. All of a sudden C 1 and C 2 attack him and accuse him of spying in their cave and pretend to tie him to a tree. All the time C 4 has been watching intently and together with C 1 he asks if the therapist likes it; whether he does not mind; C 3 looks rather puzzled. Next, C 1 gives the order for them all to leave together to really execute the task. The spy can be tried later on.

Reflection and self-criticism

During the second phase we observed some signs of appreciation, which can be looked upon as a beginning of reflection. The children feel an increasing need for this during the last phase of the therapy. Most children moreover appear capable of occasionally transcending pre-verbal realisation at the end of a game or part of a game because they formulate their experiences, wishes and appreciations. From a therapeutic point of view this is of great importance, because a reflexive moment at a higher functional level is built in between impulse and action by means of practice.

Since this is only a nascent possibility, which can admittedly speed up development, and is as yet built on a fragile foundation, the new 'moment' should therefore be applied with great caution. So consciously verbal, reflecting appreciation is not frequently found. It can only be used if the situation calls for it, if the group members' level is high enough and if they are in the mood for it. Besides, a means must be found in that case that best guarantees control over, if necessary, the termination of the happening, and the transition to a more familiar kind of action.

This was found in a variation of Corsini's 'behind the back'-technique (1957). Corsini has a member of an adult therapy group leave the circle and sit down with his back to the other members, if necessary separated from the group by a screen or wall, in such a way that visual contact is interrupted, but auditory contact is not. Then the group discusses this 'present-absent' member, by talking about the positive and negative aspects of his or her contributions and the way in which these are made.

During the last phase of structuring group therapy the following variation was applied. The children and the therapist sit down in a circle and if there are no volunteers the therapist picks out a child who will be judged by the group. The children are aware that they will all have their turn. The child in question is allowed to sit down outside the circle but is not forced to do so. The only limitation imposed on him is that he may not speak till another one has been picked out. The therapist leads the conversation. One by one the other children may give their verdict on the game and the contribution to it by the child who is being evaluated. The therapist's task in this is manifold: in a suggestive and heuristic way he supports their formulations, both by helping the children to form their sentences and with what they want to say; he ratifies realistic, positive comments; he ensures that they are objective and at the same time mild, by separating essential from emotional aspects; his attitude is neutral when he reacts to unrealistic negative utterances and he manages to put these right by reducing them to their normal proportions without frustrating the children; and the moment he thinks one of them can no longer cope with the situation he contrives to make the discussion resemble planning for further play or a subsequent session.

Such a discussion requires a fair amount of analytic power and an incipient objectivity. It will be clear that very young children will not get that far. But with those who are somewhat older, seven to eight years of age, a reasonable to good performance develops after the first or second time. The importance of this cannot be emphasized enough. The obligation to analyse more keenly play, play relations and role realisations, which is necessary for good verbalisation, has a great impact on performance during following games. When this technique has been applied a few times, we can observe an essential increase in play level, resulting from a more level-headed approach.

Once in a while reflexion on performances will lead to self-criticism. This does not mean an awareness of the good sides of their personality, as happens during adolescence, but rather a fairly vague understanding that they are different from others.

(BK2, session 26). After the game has finished C 2 keeps hanging round the therapist, while the others go to the car. All at once she asks: 'Could I have a private talk with you one of these days?' The therapist suggests that the girl might like to drop in on an evening. 'Any idea what to do?' he continues. C 2 says that she wants to tell him something. When the opportunity presents itself that evening, C 2 says after some preliminary chit-chat: 'Now I know why I come and play with you!' And seeing the therapist's puzzled expression she continues: 'I never got on well with other kids, but now you're teaching us'.

This girl has clearly reached the second treatment phase before the therapy period is actually finished. In cottage and school group her behavior is observed to have changed; it is characterized by calming down and formalisation. The majority of children need an extra treatment and consolidation period in a cottage group at the end of therapy, before this second treatment phase will be reached.

5. REMAINING QUESTIONS

Two essential questions arise following these content aspects: what happens to children who still lack sufficient structure after thirty sessions? Next: what changes or results, if any, are observed outside the therapy group? The latter issue cannot be raised till the results of experimental research of structuring group therapy have been discussed in volume II. As far as the first question is concerned, the following can be observed.

On the whole, the treatment of children who could not benefit enough from the first thirty sessions is continued, using structuring group therapy. Once their group has been dissolved they are included in new groups. So a second series of therapy sessions follows. At most this can be extended up to a total of approximately eighty sessions (one school-year), the first

103

therapy group included. Of the 30% for whom one therapy period was not enough, about 40 to 50% may benefit from continuation. The others remain a problem because treatment does not have success. They can best be regarded as a new remaining group.

In general, children of the chaotic sub-type are the major problem. However, this type is not frequently met. Furthermore, treatment is successful with some of them if the therapy described is carried out in an even more simplified way. Although they do not reach the kind of behavior described in the second phase, the lack of intentionality is seen to disappear. Thus treatment will be more successful once they have been included as asthenic structopathic children in a second therapy group.

A child who does not react positively to the treatment as an individual in a group will be faced with a similar problem to that of a child who is sure not to go on to the next class at the end of the school-year. He cannot keep up with the others, does not benefit from the therapy any more and tends to become a drag on the group's progress. Sometimes it may be necessary and possible to transfer him to another group, but solutions within the group are also possible. Eventually he may even catch up with the rest. The practical problem with the child who responds too little to treatment is the absence of creative play development. Here we get to the core of the problem: failing creativity is symptomatic of a lack of development of the structopathic child's disturbed functions. What the therapists are confronted with is: how to achieve the child's constant participation in the game. He cannot understand the developing creativity of the other children or fulfil any creative role. Apart from this, his functioning activities cannot always be integrated into the others' play. Inactivity, boredom and discomfort are likely to develop, which may lead to destructuring.

A solution is found in distinguishing two aspects of creative role-playing. On the one hand the role involves a relationship, on the other hand it has a creative content. It is now quite possible to abandon the latter aspect and to create a role which consists of a highly-functioning relationship. If, for instance, three of the four children are playing a creative game with clearly distinct roles, the non-performing child may serve as a link. As a 'child' he can be ordered to do some shopping or odd jobs, similarly he can be stimulated as a 'nurse' in a hospital and as a 'maid' at home. As an 'assistant mechanic' he can drive cars, change wheels, drive the breakdown van, take his customers home, etc. Note that the role of this child is labeled, but no creative performance is expected. All he does is to perform tasks which he is frequently 'ordered' to do. Constant stimulation is very important.

This is not merely a method to get us out of the impasse. What we aim at is stimulation of creativity, while departing from this pre-creative physical participation in a creative happening. This proves to be successful in 50% of the cases. It is a favorable coincidence that participation in the group leads to prevention of stresses, instead of a lapse into discomfort in functioning or a disturbance of the group happening. Only occasionally will such a rapid maturing occur that the child can catch up with his own first therapy group. Placement in a following group is generally needed to achieve satisfactory results.

6. EXPERIMENTAL TESTING

In this volume we have discussed a new approach to the treatment of disturbed children. Our ideas are not merely based on individual diagnostics, nor on current personality theories, which are often generalizations of a specific approach with a limited applicability. The search for adequate treatment methods departs from the 'demand', expressed by the client in his behavior in the real-life situation. The 'answer' is a first grade strategy, turning the full life situation into a treatment situation. This is a 'socio-therapeutic method'. When we succeed in making the client's 'demand' and the sociotherapist's answer, or to put it differently, disturbance type and first grade strategy, into an integrated and harmonious entity, we speak of a sociotherapeutic treatment type.

Structopathic children are a – preliminary – sociotherapeutic treatment type. In the preceding chapters we have described the disturbance type and the first grade strategy, and then the second grade strategies. We have also discussed the particular second grade strategy, structuring group therapy, at length.

There is no point in introducing new approaches if their accuracy is not demonstrated. Far too many people have already built 'castles in the air' full of treatment theories. In the introduction to this chapter, we told how we subjected our ideas to clinical tests for three years. We found it better to proceed with our tests, both for the sake of the children involved in treatment and for science. Only experimental testing of the treatment and its results would yield sufficient guarantees and evidence. This testing had to be done in the actual treatment situation and not in laboratory situations, where completely irrelevant details are often examined. Such a plan may restrict the ideal research method for the sake of the substantial and practical usefulness of the results.

Treatment as a whole is a very complicated matter. When research is started, and the number of assistants and the budget prove to be limited, we must temporize. We chose structuring group therapy for our first topic. In a project which took three years we systematically collected data which were statistically analysed. The planning, execution and results of this research require detailed discussion, so that we shall have to deal with them in the next volume. Obviously the two volumes, the one on description, the other on research, are so closely connected that they ought to be considered, read and evaluated as one study. We hope that further research will clarify the results of other aspects and consequently of the first grade strategy. These will be published in later studies.

Appendices

APPENDIX I. LIST OF THE CHILDREN WHO PARTICIPATED IN THE EXPERIMENTAL GROUPS

Column 1: *serial number*
Column 2: *code with which the child was registered*
Column 3: *sex*
Column 4: *age at the start of the structuring group therapy*
Column 5: *sub-group in which the child is included; s = sthenic; a = asthenic; ch = chaotic*
Column 6: *+ = child welfare child*
Column 7: *e = emotional neglect was a contributory factor; b = neglect in up-bringing was a contributory factor*

Column 8: *+ = just before treatment started the child was in his own, complete family; 1 = idem, but only one parent present at home; F = before admission the child was with foster-parents*
Column 9: *x = one of the parents is reputed to be 'disturbed'; (x) = the absent parent was diagnosed as such; m = one of the parents is mentally defective.*

1	2	3	4	5	6	7	8	9
1	AK6–1	b	9;2	s	—	—	+	—
2	AK6–2	b	10;10	s	—	—	+	—
3	AK6–3	b	10;2	a	—	—	+	—
4	AK6–4	b	10;10	a	—	—	+	—
5	AK9–1	g	10;1	a	—	—	+	—
6	AK9–2	g	9;7	s	—	—	+	—
7	AK9–3	g	10;1	a	—	—	+	—
8	AK9–4	g	10;3	s	—	—	+	—
9	BK1–1	g	7;4	s	—	—	+	—
10	BK1–2	g	7;8	a	—	—	+	—
11	BK1–3	g	8;2	a	—	—	+	—
12	BK2–1	g	9;9	a	—	—	+	—
13	BK2–2	g	8;7	s	—	—	+	—
14	BK2–3	g	9;2	s	—	—	+	—
15	BK2–4	g	9;2	a	—	—	+	—
16	BK4–1	g	8;0	a	—	—	+	—
17	BK4–2	g	8;1	s	+	e	F	—

1	2	3	4	5	6	7	8	9
18	BK4–3	g	8;3	s	+	e	F	−
19	BK4–4	g	8;6	s	+	e	1	(x)
20	BK5–1	g	9;5	s	−	−	1	−
21	BK5–2	g	10;2	s	−	−	1	(x)
22	BK5–3	g	10;5	ch	−	−	+	−
23	BK5–4	g	9;7	a	−	−	+	−
24	MK3–1	b	8;4	a	−	−	+	−
25	MK3–2	b	7;8	s	−	−	+	−
26	MK3–3	b	9;0	s	−	−	F	−
27	MK3–4	b	8;9	a	−	−	+	−
28	RB1–1	b	7;11	ch	−	−	1	x
29	RB1–2	b	9;2	a	−	−	+	−
30	RB1–3	b	8;0	s	−	e	+	−
31	RD1–1	g	5;9	a	−	−	+	−
32	RD1–2	b	5;4	s	−	−	+	x
33	RD1–3	b	6;0	a	−	−	+	−
34	RD3–1	b	10;0	a	−	−	+	−
35	RD3–2	b	8;1	a	−	−	+	−
36	RD3–3	b	8;3	a	−	−	1	−
37	RD3–4	b	6;10	s	−	−	+	−
38	RK7–1	g	8;5	ch	−	−	+	−
39	RK7–2	b	9;0	a	−	−	+	x
40	RK7–3	b	8;0	ch	−	−	+	−
41	RK8–1	b	7;11	ch	−	−	+	−
42	RK8–2	b	8;2	ch	−	−	+	−
43	RK8–3	b	8;1	ch	−	e	+	−
44	RV1–1	b	9;2	a	−	−	+	−
45	RV1–2	b	10;5	a	−	−	+	−
46	RV1–3	b	8;6	s	−	−	+	−
47	RV2–1	b	5;7	s	−	e	F	x
48	RV2–2	g	7;7	ch	−	−	+	−
49	RV2–3	b	6;3	s	+	b	+	m
50	RV6–1	g	8;7	a	−	−	+	−
51	RV6–2	g	9;11	a	−	−	+	−
52	RV6–3	b	9;11	s	−	−	1	−
53	RV6–4	b	9;0	a	−	−	+	−

APPENDIX II. DESCRIPTION OF THE CHILDREN FROM THREE EX-
PERIMENTAL THERAPY GROUPS (BK2 – MK3 – RD1) WHO ARE
USED AS EXAMPLES IN CHAPTER 6

A. Group BK2

C1 is an asthenic structopathic girl, 9;9 at the start of the therapy group.
She is the third child of a pleasant family of five children. Normal grav-

idity, difficult partus, pylorospasm, xerosis, dystrophia. When three months old she was operated on for pylorospasm. Noisy baby, difficult infant. She is characterized by nagging, inability to play and what her mother calls: lack of instinct. In kindergarten she becomes a problem child, who irritates other children because of unadapted reactions (slightly hysteriform) and she gradually becomes a scapegoat. When $4\frac{1}{2}$ she suffers from a serious attack of measles (encephalitis) and on the whole is susceptible to infectious diseases (also several times otitis media). At the end of the kindergarten period she stays in a vacation camp for six months. In primary school she is a poor-to-mediocre pupil with very fluctuating performance. Socially, she turns out to be more and more unadapted. When 7;4 she is molested by a group of children from the neighborhood when leaving school; she is knocked down and dragged along the street. Afterwards she is in a state of shock and appears to have a commotio cerebri. When 8;1 she is placed in a sociotherapeutic treatment center. Examination: choreatiform hyperactivity, disturbed reflexes, vegetative lability, immature EEG. Diffuse cerebral disturbances owing to a neurasthenic constitution, followed by encephalopathy. Psychology tests: Terman IQ 98, SON (a Dutch intelligence test of the performance type, initially developed for deaf children) 106, both with considerable divergence; analytic perception weak. Retarded and somewhat weak attention span; perseverations of set. Infantile personality with hysteriform traits. Before her therapy group starts (this group is the first experimental group) she has been in the center for 20 months. She calms down slightly during these months but continues to display the same irritating behavior, but in a milder form now, alternated with vehement eruptions. Both in cottage and school group she becomes a queer individual, incurring the angry reactions and mockery from the other group members. Her complete lack of progress is characterized by the group workers as: 'she doesn't improve or get on'.

C2 is a sthenic structopathic girl of 8;7, rather tall for her age. She is the third child from a good family with four daughters. Rhesus-child, exsanguinized. Cute baby, developing noisy and difficult behavior during early infancy. As an infant she is troublesome and aggressive. Very insufficient frustration tolerance. Constantly at odds with sisters and girlfriends; quarrels and fights are a daily occurrence. In primary school she performs well in spite of her short attention span; nevertheless she is socially unfit for school. Again and again she disturbs the lessons, becomes wilful and impudent and she is always up to mischief. In the neighborhood she is the scapegoat who is blamed for all nasty things that occur. She becomes a highly suspicious outcast, who becomes aggressive at the slightest provocation. The family, specifically her mother, are considerably vexed by this. The headmaster advices that she be sent to a 'strict' boarding-school once she has finished the first year. When the established regime appears to fail and she is in danger of losing confidence, even after a few months, she is sent back home. When 7;11 she is placed in a sociotherapeutic treatment center via a child guidance clinic. Examination: choreatiform hyperactivity, increased reflexes, EEG's normal. Psychology tests: Terman IQ 127, Wisc verbal 123, performance 116 due to weak analytic perception. Bourdon – Wiersma: great pace, no omissions, fluctuating performance, especially as regards erroneous crossings out. Projection examination: infantile personality with good but neither integrated nor controlled emotional possibilities, suspicious and aggressive, shock reactions. She is still insufficiently lateralized (note: she never had any reading difficulties). During the eight months in the center before the therapy group starts she is a problem girl who keeps exhibiting the phenomena described. The cottage group is badly influenced by her because she is soon to gain structural leadership, especially through intimidation, which she uses against the staff.

C3 and C4 are monozygotic twins of 9;2, who display sthenic and asthenic structopathic behavior respectively. They are the fifth and sixth children in a family of ten. Partus was premature ($7\frac{1}{2}$ months), weights 2050 and 2140 grams respectively; incubator. Convulsions during the first years. Polyclinic inspection. Deviating EEG's tending to epilepsy. In kindergarten problems arise especially with C3, who has disturbing aggressive behavior. But C4 gives problems as well: she is not very active, she hardly participates in anything; she is suspected of being sneaky. Primary school soon mentions similar problems. C4 has petit-mal phenomena to a slight degree. The school performance of both is mediocre and highly fluctuating. Meanwhile medication has been started. The child guidance clinic offers the children to a sociotherapeutic treatment center where they are placed when 8;4. Examination: medical data as above. Psychology tests: C3: Terman IQ 109, SON 111, block design and design completion poor. Attention span clearly disturbed: retarded, drops in consciousness; epileptic symptoms. Infantile and rather poor personality; dominant and aggressive; many perseverations. C4: Terman IQ 111, SON 114, weak analytic perception and motor component. Attention span: see C3. Infantile and rather poor personality; somewhat resigned kindness, feelings of inferiority, slight formalism. During the ten months in the center before the therapy group starts C3 causes many problems and complaints. Unlike her mother, group workers and psychologists alike consider her more difficult and problematic than C4. She wants to dominate but cannot achieve this because she is not able to; this makes her very irritable. When 8;11 she has an insultus at home after an infectious disease (no repetitions). C4 is easier to talk to and she flourishes slightly, although it remains difficult to establish proper contact with her and to make her participate in group events. She takes things lying down without being unkind. At regular intervals she has retarded explosive reactions to frustrations.

B. Group MK3

C1 is an asthenic structopathic boy, 8;4 at the start of the therapy. He is the oldest of three children and comes from a quiet, good family. Partus was difficult; asphyxia. Initial development is severely retarded. When five months old: dystrophia. Susceptible to infectious diseases. Difficult and troublesome infant, weak, poor eater, whimsical, avital and full of discomfort, vehement eruptions of rage which sometimes cannot be traced back to stresses. He cannot play and he is in constant trouble with other children. In primary school the situation becomes untenable, after constant complaints had been received from kindergarten. He is classified as a troublesome, mentally defective boy. Psychological examination rules out debilitas. When 7;10, after a long waiting-period, he is placed in a treatment center. Examination: serious degree of choreatiform hyperactivity, increased reflexes and irritability, slight tremor, slight neuropathic constitution. Diffuse cerebral pathology owing to minimal brain damage during partus. Immature EEG. Psychology tests: Terman IQ 118; Wisc verbal 124, performance 120 with great divergence at the expense of visual-analytic perception and motor realization. Fluctuating attention span with spasmodic compensatory attempts to regulate. Chaotic infantile personality, no integration, constantly losing his temper; slightly formalistic superstructure; formalism. In the center, before the start of the therapy, he is a queer and lonely figure, who cannot bear contact, but is repeatedly at variance with others.

C2 is a sthenic structopathic boy; he is 7;8 when the group starts. He is the youngest of three children from a normal family. Rhesus child, exsanguinized several times. During (early) infancy his noisy and impetuous behavior is striking. Strongly losing his temper; 'unreasonable', the parents say. Twice he is expelled from kindergarten and stays at home for a considerable time, where he always manages to have his way using

111

pressure, and outbursts of rage. His mother can no longer manage him. The first class turns out to be a downright failure; he attacks his school-teacher and the other children, bullies the community, defies measures taken by the headmaster and outside he fights both big and small. Within two months' time he is expelled from school. He is placed in a treatment center by the medical authorities. Examination: serious degree of choreatiform hyperactivity, almost similar to chorea minor. EEG normal for his age; no further neurological deviations. From a psychiatric point of view, a very primitive child, whose life is pure passion. He is in danger of becoming a very aggressive psychopath if his behavior cannot be modified with the aid of a consistent approach. Psychology test: Wisc verbal 98, performance 107, great disharmony, combination and memory good, analytic perception extremely weak. Bourdon – Wiersma could not be taken. Impression of marked drops in energy. During the four months he is in the center, before the therapy group starts, he is unmanageable; the more so because he is a strong boy with brutal physical power. Especially in school conflicts occur frequently. Problems get less in the cottage group when crises are solved by giving in to him somewhat when he partly obeys an order. He continues to suffer from enuresis.

C3 is a sthenic structopathic boy, 9;0 when the group starts. He is the son of an unmarried mother with severe psychiatric disturbances; when he is 3 months old he is adopted by foster-parents. In this family his development is retarded and gives problems. Linguistic progress is severely retarded: at five he can only speak a few words with great difficulty. When he displays severe behavior disorders in primary school and shortly afterwards in the special class, he is placed in a sociotherapeutic treatment center at the age of 8;0. Examination: anamnesic data about gravidity and partus cannot be traced; we only know that birth took place under very primitive circumstances. His chorea minor can be traced back to minimal brain damage during partus. Physical neglect during the first month cannot be ruled out. Further diagnostic data: dysdiadochokinesis, deviating Babinsky's, right stronger than left, dilated ventricles at the expense of the left side, clearly deviating EEG, tending to epilepsy, centrencephalic. Psychology tests: Terman IQ 83, SON 92, retentive memory, combination normal, block design and design completion poor. Highly disturbed consciousness regulation, retarded, great drops. A chaotic, clinging personality, slight social-emotional development, diffuse-global perception so that he has little hold on reality. Strongly dominated by comfort-discomfort. During the first year of placement there is hardly any rise in level. He remains a sluggish, aggressive boy with strong

112

perseverations; it is difficult to keep him from negative reactions; he feels frustrated because of his discomfort. He has no understanding of the situations and behavior of others and he shows inadequate and rigid reactions, characterized by tenacious, inert outbursts of losing his temper. At regular intervals he flies into a rage, especially if he is crossed in any way: he lies down, screams and yells till he loses his voice, kicking and punching with arms and legs till exhaustion forces him to stop. In such a case it is difficult to approach him in any way and he lacks all contact with the outside world. There is nothing left to do but stay with him and soothe him. He needs sedatives.

C4 is an asthenic structopathic boy, 8;9 when the therapy group starts. He comes from a good family and is the oldest of three children. Difficult partus, pylorospasm, intoxication, dystrophia. Commotio cerebri when he is 9 months old. A great many infections, sinusitis and pleurisy. At the age of six, kidney and liver complaints. He is a problem child, who misses a lot at school due to ill-health. This cannot, however, account for his difficulties with other children in the neighborhood and in school. He causes trouble, it is as if he actually wants to be the butt of teasings, which results in serious frustration. For days on end he will remain sullen and obstinate. Though his parents help him kindly and try to explain the outcome of his unadapted behavior, he continues to exhibit 'stupid and strange' reactions. If he enjoys something he gets completely beside himself; then it is no longer possible to get any hold on him. He displays infantile behavior, is exuberant, hyperactive and seems to have lost contact with his environment. When 8;2 he leaves for a vacation-camp where he stays for half a year. Here too he is a striking, somewhat elusive boy who causes conflicts once he feels settled. The management reports that these problems are difficult to remove because they are not due to direct aggressiveness but are imperceptibly caused, so that they can only take action when it is too late. Almost directly after coming home he is placed in a sociotherapeutic treatment center. Examination: early neurological damage due to xerosis, post-traumatic encephalopathy, asthenic feminine structure, choreatiform hyperactivity, Babinsky left pathological. Psychology tests: Terman IQ 116, slightly incoherent, lacks functional flexibility; SON 134, memory and combination very good, serial ordering mediocre, block designs and design completion relatively poor. Concentration from rigid to fluctuating; reasonable, slightly retarded performance during short spells of rigid superstructure control. At first a seemingly encapsulated formalistic personality, very rapidly off his balance, resulting in infantile, diffuse, sometimes chaotic, sometimes

113

strangely original reactions. During the weeks in the center just before the therapy group starts the behavior difficulties mentioned have come to a head, though during the first two days his behavior was very quiet.

C. Group RD1

C1 is an asthenic structopathic girl, 5;9 when her therapy group starts. At the age of 5;7 she is offered for placement in a sociotherapeutic treatment center; labeled a psychopath. She is the oldest of two children from a good family. Partus 14 days overdue, Sturzgeburt. Noisy baby, troublesome infant. At the age of $3\frac{1}{2}$ she develops parotitis followed by meningitis and lung tuberculosis. For the latter she is treated for one year. Physical development is clearly retarded; unmanageable when home again. By nagging and bullying she starts to threaten her mother; sadistic behavior towards younger brother. Constant quarrels with other children in the neighborhood. Behavior deviations are viewed by the parents as abnormal and terrifying. Examination: severe choreatiform hyperactivity. Bilateral Babinsky's. Diffuse motor disturbances. Diffuse subcortical and cortical disturbances owing to minimal brain damage during partus and neurotoxical damage. Psychology tests: Terman IQ 97, divergence 4;0 – 7;0, little interiorized, very childish, series of both sensorial and motor sets of perseveration. SON 81, very restless and immature when performing tasks, should be able to have a greater performance, block design weak. Attention span highly fluctuating, drops in energy. Very infantlike girl, has no control whatsoever, chaotic and restless. During the two months in the center before the therapy group starts, her short spells of lack of vitality are striking: strong persevering functioning is alternated by spells of restless and noisy behavior, which soon frustrates her. She then panics immediately, screaming, scratching, cursing and uttering not quite intelligible reproaches. It takes quite a long time before she comes to her senses; exhaustion changes the picture.

C2 is a sthenic structopathic boy, 5;4 when the therapy group starts. The oldest from a family of two children; labile mother who received psychiatric treatment for some time because of pregnancy psychosis. His partus was premature and difficult (8 months); anoxia. Noisy baby, very passionate and troublesome infant. Clearly exudative child; bronchitis, sinusitis, otitis media, diarrhoea and vomiting, headaches. Constantly losing his temper after which he turns blue. A persistent faeces-eater; keeps suffering from enuresis. From an early age he is always quarreling, fighting – punching and kicking – with his brother and children in the street. He kicks

114

up rows without any apparent reason; is very destructive, consequently the scapegoat of the neighborhood. Adult neighbors punish him by beating him, which only makes him more cunning and aggressive. In kindergarten he is completely unmanageable. Via the psychiatric department of the health authorities he is offered to a sociotherapeutic treatment center when 5;2. Examination: bilateral deviating Babinsky's, lanugo pilosis, second and third toes have grown together; EEG's: central sub-cortical disturbances (epilepsy), also anomalies left temporal. Psychology tests: Terman IQ 121; SON 135, block design and design completion weak. Attention span on the whole good, great pace, clear relapses. Severely retarded social-emotional development. Perception is diffuse and too global. Strong assertiveness. During the first weeks in the center he is a boy with primarily aggressive reactions and because of his intelligence it is practically impossible to get any hold on him. The other children are not safe with him; he smashes the common room, the furniture and the toys.

C3 is an asthenic structopathic boy, 6;0 when the therapy group starts. He is the oldest of a simple, normal family with two children. Disturbed gravidity: diabetes and anaemia. Partus a-term. After six weeks dystrophia; he only vomits, does not take any food, considerable loss of weight. He is treated by a pediatrician. At the age of 2½ gastro-enteritis. Shortly afterwards bilateral otitis media. Severely retarded linguistic development. At the age of 3 he utters the first word. (When he is offered for treatment he speaks only very little and then defectively). Difficult infant. Often losing his temper. He fails to play and establish contact. Often fighting and quarreling with other infants. No insight into situations. When 5;8 he has an attack of croup. When 5;10 he is put down for the sociotherapeutic treatment center by a polyclinic. Examination: asymmetric skull, serious degree of choreatiform hyperactivity, dysdiadochokinesis, pathological Babinsky right, very poor co-ordination. Pathological EEG's; first time: highly asymmetric basic rhythm at the expense of the left side, focal pathology is not clear; second time: pathology temporal right, also disturbance in the left background activity; suspicious that epilepsy is developing. Diffusely neurological disturbance, perinatal, prenatal subcortical damage and post-natal dystrophia. Psychology tests: Terman IQ 88 with basic 3½; disturbance in linguistic development; similarities at the age of 7 positive. SON IQ 116, very disharmonic, block design and design completion very poor, as well as serial ordering. Disturbed attention span: inactive consciousness and clear drops. Primitive infant, without norms, egocentric, diffuse global perception. During the first months in the center his behavior is reactive-aggressive. When contact with adults is not desired he avoids it by secluding himself; if he experiences it positively he becomes very elated. In the cottage group he is soon off his balance since he has no idea of what is happening.

References

Aichhorn, A., *Verwahrloste Jugend*, Bern, 1957[4]
Allen, F.H., *Psychotherapy with children*, New York, 1942
Allport, G.W., Psychological models for guidance, in: Mosher, R.L. a.o. (eds.): *Guidance: an examination*, New York, p. 13–23, 1965
Alt, H., *Residential treatment for the disturbed child*, New York, 1960
Asperger, H., *Heilpädagogik*, Vienna, 1956[2]
Axline, V.M., *Play therapy, The inner dynamics of childhood*, Cambridge-Massachusetts, 1947

Bach, G.R., *Intensive group psychotherapy*, New York, 1954
Bales, R.F., *Interaction process analysis. A method for the study of small groups*, Cambridge, 1951
Bales, R.F. a.o., Channels of communication in small groups, in: *Am. Sociol. Rev.*, XVI, p. 461–468, 1951
Bandura, A., Behavior modification through modelling procedures, in: Krasner, L., Ullmann, L.P. (eds.): *Research in behavior modification*, New York, 1965
Bandura, A., Walters, R.H., *Social learning and personality development*, New York, 1967[2]
Bennis, W.G., Benne, K.D., Chin, R. (eds.), *The planning of change. Readings in the applied behavioral sciences*, New York, 1961
Bennis, W.G., Shepard, H.A., A theory of group development, in: Bennis, W.G., Benne, K.D., Chin, R. (eds.): *The planning of change. Readings in the applied behavioral sciences*, New York, p. 321–340, 1961
Berkowitz, L., The development of motives and values in the child, in: *Basic Topics in Psychology*, New York, 1964[2]
Bettelheim, B., *Love is not enough, The treatment of emotionally disturbed children*, Glencoe, Illinois, 1952[4]

Cartwright, D., Lippitt, R., Group dynamics and the individual, in: Bennis, W.G., Benne, K.D., Chin, R. (eds.): *The planning of change, Readings in the applied behavioral sciences*, New York, p. 264–277, 1961
Cartwright, D., Zander, A. (eds.), *Group dynamics, Research and theory*, New York, 1960[2]
Clarke, J., Delinquent personalities, in: *The Brit. J. of Criminology*, III, p. 147–161, 1962–63
Coch, R., French, J.R.P., Overcoming resistance to change, in: *Human Relations*, p. 512–532, 1948

117

Cohen, R.S., Therapeutic education and day treatment: a new professional liaison, in: *Except. Children*, XXXII, p. 23–28, 1965
Cohen, A.R., Attitude change and social influence, in: *Basic Topics in Psychology*, New York, 1967[3]
Corsini, R.J., *Methods of group psychotherapy*, New York, 1957
Corsini, R.J., *Roleplaying in psychotherapy. A manual*, Chicago, 1966
Cousinet, R., *La vie sociale des enfants*, Paris, 1959
Crocket, R., Authority and permissiveness in the psychotherapeutic community: theoretical perspectives, in: *Am. J. of Psychotherapy*, XX, p. 669–676, 1966
Cronbach, L.J., *Essentials of psychological testing*, New York, 1960[2]
Cruickshank, W.M., *The brain-injured child in home, school, and community*, New York, 1967

Dabrowski, K., *Positive disintegration*, Boston, 1964
Dührssen, A., *Psychotherapie bei Kindern und Jugendlichen. Biographische Anamnese und therapeutische Verfahren*, Göttingen, 1960

Edelson, M., *Sociotherapy and psychotherapy*, Chicago, 1970
Edelson, M., *The practice of sociotherapy. A case study*, New Haven-London, 1970
Edwards, A.L., *Techniques of attitude scale construction*, New York, 1957
Edwards, A.L., Experiments: their planning and execution, in: Lindzey, G. (ed.), *Handbook of social psychology*, Vol. I, London, p. 259–288, 1959[3]
Elms, A.C. (ed.), *Roleplaying, reward and attitude change*, New York, 1969
Eysenck, H.J., Rachman, S., *The causes and cures of neurosis*, London, 1965

Faure, J.L., Le sentiment d'abandon chez l'enfant, in: *Sauvegarde de l'enfance*, p. 5–6 1952
Festinger, L., Katz, D. (eds.), *Research methods in the behavioral sciences*, New York, 1966
Flanagan, J.C., The critical incident technique, in: *Psychol. Bulletin*, LI, p. 327–358, 1954
Flavell, J.H., *The development of role-taking and communication skills in children*, New York, 1968
Fraiberg, S.H., *The magic years. Understanding the problems of early childhood*, London, 1968
Freeman, F.S., *Theory and practice of psychological testing*, New York, 1962[3]
Freud, A., *Einführung in die Technik der Kinderanalyse*, Munich, 1964[4]
Friedlander, K., *The psychoanalytical approach to juvenile delinquency*, New York, 1947
Frye, I.B.M., Erziehungsschwierigkeiten bei emotionell Verwahrlosten, in: Ebermaier, C.: *Das schwererziehbare Kind*, Düsseldorf, 1959

Galtung, J., *Theory and methods of social research*, London, 1969[2]
Giffin, M., The role of child psychiatry in learning disabilities, in: Myklebust, H.R. (ed.): *Progress in learning disabilities*, Vol. I, New York, p. 75–97, 1968
Gill, H.S., The 'therapeutic community' as an approach to psychotherapy, in: *Psychotherapy: theory, research and practice*, IV, p. 87–91, 1967
Ginott, H.G., *Group psychotherapy with children. The theory and practice of play therapy*, New York, 1961
Goldstein, K., *The organism*, New York, 1939
Goldstein, K., *After effects of brain injuries in war*, New York, 1942

Groot, A.D. de, *Methodology*, The Hague-Holland, 1969
Guilford, J.P., *Psychometric methods*, New York, 1954[2]
Guilford, J.P., Jorgersen, A.P., Some constant errors in ratings, in: *J. of Exp. Psychol.*, XXII, p. 43–57, 1938

Hare, R.D., *Psychopathy, Theory and research*, New York, 1970
Haring, N.G., Phillips, E.L., *Educating emotionally disturbed children*, New York, 1962
Hart de Ruyter, Th., Boeke, P.E., Beugen, M. van, *Het moeilijk opvoedbare kind in het pleeggezin. Een behandelingsmethode voor kinderen met ernstige gedragsstoornissen*, Assen-Holland, 1968. (The child with severe behavior disorders in the foster-home. A method of treatment for children with severe behavior disorders)
Haufmann, E., Social structure of a group of Kindergarten children, in: Charters, W.; Gage, N. (eds.): *Readings in the social psychology of education*, Boston, p. 123–125, 1963
Haworth, M.R. (ed.), *Child psychotherapy: Practice and theory*, London, 1964
Heyns, R.W.; Lippitt, R., Systematic observational techniques, in: Lindzey, G. (ed.), *Handbook of social psychology*, Vol. I, London, p. 370–404, 1959[3]
Heyns, R.W.; Zander, A.F., Observation of group behavior, in: Festinger, L.; Katz, D. (eds.), *Research methods in the behavioral sciences*, New York, 1966
Huessy, H.R., Study of the prevalence and therapy of the choreatiform syndrome or hyperkinesis in Rural Vermont, in: *Acta Paedopsychiatrica*, XXXIV, p. 130–135, 1967
Hugenholtz, P.Th., *Tijd en creativiteit. Ontwerp van een structurele anthropologie*, Amsterdam, 1959 (Time and creativity. Concept of a structural anthropology)

Jones, M., Towards a clarification of the 'therapeutic community' concept, in: *Brit. J. of Medical Psychology*, XXXII, p. 200–205, 1959
Jones, M., *Beyond the therapeutic community*, London, 1968

Kaiser, C.A., Group work, in: Peck, H.B. (ed.): The group in education, group work and psychotherapy, in: *Am. J. of Orthopsychiatry*, XXIV, p. 129–133, 1954
Kelly, G.A., *The psychology of personal constructs*, New York, 1955
Kelly, E.L., Fiske, D.W., The prediction of success in the V A training program in clinical psychology, in: *Am. Psychologist*, V, p. 395–406, 1950
Kendall, M.G., *Rank correlation methods*, London, 1953
Klein, J., *Working with groups*, London, 1966[3]
Klein, M., *La psychanalyse des enfants*, P.U.F., Paris, 1959
Konopka, G., *Social group work*. Prentice-Hall, 1964
Krasner, L., Ullmann, L.P. (eds.), *Research in behavior modification*, New York, 1965
Krech, D., Crutchfield, R.S., *Theory and problems of social psychology*, New York, 1948
Krevelen, D.A. van, Klinische 24-Stunden-Therapie bei neurotischen Kindern und Jugendlichen, in: *Acta Paedopsychiatrica*, XXXIV, p. 251–273, 1967
Kritzer, H., Philips, C.A., Observing group psychotherapy – an affective learning experience, in: *Am. J. of Psychotherapy*, XX, p. 471, 1966

Lam, R.L. 't, Bepaling en interpretatie van vier cognitieve dimensies, in: *Gawein*, XIV, p. 119–167, 1965 (Determination and interpretation of four cognitive dimensions)

119

Langeveld, M.J., Das Ding in der Welt des Kindes, in: *Studien zur Anthropologie des Kindes*, Tübingen, 1956

Lesemann, G., Ordnung heilt – Heilung ordnet. Zur Rückfindung zum Grundsätzlichen in der Heilpädagogik, in: *Zs. f. Heilpädagogik*, XVII, p. 97–109, 1966

Levit, G., Jennings, H.H., Learning through roleplaying, in: Bennis, W.G., Benne, K.D., Chin, R. (eds.), *The planning of change. Readings in the applied behavioral sciences*, New York, p. 706–710, 1961

Lewin, K., Frontiers in group dynamics. Concept, method and reality in social science; social equilibria and social change, in: *Human relations*, p. 5–41, 1947

Lewin, K., Grabbe, P., Principles of re-education, in: Bennis, W.G.; Benne, K.D., Chin, R. (eds.), *The planning of change. Readings in the applied behavioral sciences*, New York, p. 503–509, 1961

Lindzey, G. (ed.), *Handbook of social psychology*, Vol. I, London, 1959[3]

Llorens, L.A., Rubin, E.Z., *Developing ego functions in disturbed children. Occupational therapy in milieu*, Detroit, 1967

Maier, H.W., Group living: a unique feature in residential treatment, in: *New perspectives on services to groups. Theory, organization, practice; social work with groups*, New York, 1961

Maier, H.W. (ed.), *Group work as a part of residential treatment*, New York, 1965

Malan, D.H., *A study of brief psychotherapy*, Social science paperbacks, nr. 23, London, 1967

McClure, A.G., Reaction types in maladjusted children, in: Haworth, M.R. (ed.): *Child psychotherapy. Practice and theory*, London, p. 45–50, 1964

McQuitty, L., Elementary linkage analysis for isolating orthogonal and oblique types and typical relevancies, in: *Educational and psychological measurement*, Vol. XVII, p. 216, s.a.

Mesinger, J.F., Emotionally disturbed and brain damaged children – should we mix them?, in: *Exceptional Children*, XXXII, p. 237–240, 1965

Miles, M.B., The training group, in: Bennis, W.G., Benne, K.D., Chin, R. (eds.), *The planning of change. Readings in the applied behavioral sciences*, New York, p. 716–725, 1961

Moor, P., *Heilpädagogische Psychologie*, Vol. II, Bern, 1958

Moor, P., *Heilpädagogik. Ein pädagogisches Lehrbuch*, Bern, 1965

Mowrer, O.H., *Learning theory and personality dynamics*, New York, 1950

Mowrer, O.H., The behavior therapies, with special reference to modeling and imitation, in: *Am. J. of Psychotherapy*, XX, p. 439–461, 1966

Myklebust, H.R., Learning disabilities: definition and overview, in: Myklebust, H.R. (ed.): *Progress in learning disabilities*, Vol. I, New York, p. 1–15, 1968

Nickel, H., *Die visuelle Wahrnehmung in Kindergarten- und Einschulungsalter. Untersuchungen zur Frage einer einzelheitlichen Auffassung*, Stuttgart, 1967

Nooteboom, W.E., *Some psychological aspects of the choreatiform syndrome*, Assen-Holland, 1967

Olst, E.H. van; Orlebeke, J.F., An analysis of the concept of arousal, in: *Ned. Ts. Psychol.*, XXII, p. 583–603, Amsterdam, 1967

Patterson, C.H., Divergence and convergence in psychotherapy, in: *Am. J. of Psychotherapy*, XXI, p. 4–17, 1967

120

Peck, H.B. (ed.), The group in education, group work and psychotherapy, in: *Am. J. of Orthopsychiatry*, XXIV, p. 128–152, 1954

Phillips, E.L.; Wiener, D.A.; Haring, N.G., *Discipline, achievement and mental health*, Englewood Cliffs, N.J., 1960

Phillips, E.L.; Wiener, D.N., *Short-term psychotherapy and structured behavior change*, New York, 1966

Piel, W., Zum Begriff der Regression, in: Kirchhoff, H.; Pietrowicz, B.: Kontaktgestörte Kinder, in: *Psychol. Praxis*, 29, Basel, 1961

Polsky, H.W., *Cottage six. The social system of delinquent boys in residential treatment*, New York, 1963[2]

Polsky, H.W.; Claster, D.S., *The dynamics of residential treatment. A social system analysis*, Chapel Hill, 1968

Prechtl, H.F.R., *Het cerebraal gestoorde kind*, Groningen-Holland, 1963 (The child with minimal brain damage)

Rambert, M.L., *La vie affective et morale de l'enfant. Douze ans de pratique psychanalitique*, Neuchâtel, 1963[3]

Rapoport, R.N., *Community as doctor. New perspectives on a therapeutic community*, London, 1960

Redl, F., *When we deal with children. Selected writings*, New York-London, 1966

Redl, F.; Wineman, D., *Children who hate*, Glencoe, 1951

Redl, F.; Wineman, D., *Controls from within. Techniques for the treatment of the aggressive child*, Glencoe, 1960[3]

Reisman, J.M., *Toward the integration of psychotherapy*, New York, 1971

Rexford, E.N. et al., A follow-up of a psychiatric study of 57 antisocial young children, in: *Ment. Hyg.*, XL, New York, p. 196–214, 1956

Rexford, E.N. (ed.), A developmental approach to the problems of acting out. A symposium, in: *Monographs of the J. of the Am. Academy of Child Psychiatry*, nr. 1, New York, 1966

Robins, L.N., *Deviant children grown up. A sociological and psychiatric study of sociopathic personality*, Baltimore, 1966

Robinson, R.J. (ed.), *Brain and early behavior. Development in the fetus and infant*, London-New York, 1969

Rogers, C.R., *The clinical treatment of the problem child*, Boston, 1939

Rogers, C.R., *Counseling and psychotherapy*, Boston, 1942

Rogers, C.R., *Client-centered psychotherapy. Its current practice, implication and theory*, Boston, 1951

Rogers, C.R., The necessary and sufficient conditions of therapeutic personality change, in: *J. Consult. Psychol.* XXI, p. 95–103, 1957

Rogers, C.R., *On becoming a person. A therapist's view of psychotherapy*, London, 1961

Rogers, C.R.; Truax, C.B., The therapeutic conditions antecedent to change: a theoretical view, in: Rogers, C.R. (ed.): *The therapeutic relationship and its impact. A study of psychotherapy with schizophrenics*, Madison-Milwaukee, p. 97–108, 1967

Ruitenbeek, H.M. (ed.), *Group therapy today. Styles, methods, and techniques*, New York, 1969

Sandschulte, M., Tiefenpsychologie und heilpädagogische Praxis, in: *Formen und Führen; kleine Schriften zur Psychologie, Pädagogik und Heilpädagogik*, Vol. 17, Luzern, 1960

Scheidlinger, S., Group psychotherapy, in: Peck, H.B. (ed.): The group in education, group work and psychotherapy, in: *Am. J. of Orthopsychiatry*, XXIV, p. 140–145, 1954

Schiffer, M., *The therapeutic play group*, New York, 1969

Schrager, J. et al., The hyperkinetic child: some consensually validated behavioral correlates, in: *Except. Children*, XXXII, p. 635–637, 1966

Schulman, D., Openness of perception as a condition for creativity, in: *Except. Children*, XXXIII, p. 89–94, 1966

Selltiz, C., Jahoda, M., Deutsch, M., Cook, S.W., *Research methods in social relations*, New York, 1959[2]

Siegel, S. *Nonparametric statistics for the behavioral sciences*, New York, 1956

Slavson, S.R., *Child psychotherapy*, New York, 1952

Slavson, S.R., *An introduction to group therapy*, New York, 1960[7]

Smirnoff, V., *La psychanalyse de l'enfant*, P.U.F., Paris, 1966

Solomon, L.N.; Berzon, B.; Weedman, C., The programmed group: a new rehabilitation resource, in: *Int. J. of Group psychotherapy*, XVIII, p. 199–219, 1968

Spiel, W., *Die Therapie in der Kinder- und Jugendpsychiatrie*, Stuttgart, 1967

Spitz, R.A., *A genetic field theory of ego formation. Its implication for pathology*, New York, 1959

Städeli, H., Spieltherapie und Persönlichkeitsentwicklung, in: *Praxis der Kinderpsychologie und Kinderpsychiatrie*, XI, 7, p. 251–255, 1962

Sternberg, T.E., *Zur Entwicklung der mitmenschlichen Beziehungen in den ersten Lebensjahren bei Heimkindern*, Bern, 1962

Stoller, F.H., Accelerated interaction: a time-limited approach based on the brief, intensive group, in: *Int. J. of Group Psychotherapy*, XVIII, p. 220–235, 1968

Stone, F.H., The day care approach to emotionally disturbed children, in: Maxwell, S.M. (ed.): *Emotionally disturbed children. Proceedings of the annual study conference of the association of workers for maladjusted children*, London, 1966

Strauss, A.A.; Lehtinen, L.E., *Psychopathology and education of the brain-injured child*, New York, 1958[8]

Stutte, H.; Koch, H. (eds.), *Charakteropathien nach frühkindlichen Hirnschäden*, Berlin-New York, 1970

Taft, J., *The dynamics of therapy in a controlled relationship*, New York, 1933–1962

Tausch, R.; Tausch, A.M., *Kinderpsychotherapie in nicht-direktivem Verfahren*, Göttingen, 1956

Tausch, R.; Tausch, A.M., *Erziehungspsychologie. Psychologische Vorgänge in Erziehung und Unterricht*, Göttingen, 1965[2]

Traxler, A.E.; North, R.D., *Techniques of guidance*, New York, 1966[3]

Tryon, R.C., Reliability and behavior domain validity: reformulation and historical critique, in: *Psychol. Bulletin*, LIV, p. 229–249, 1957

Vass, I., The acting-out patient in group therapy, in: *Am. J. of Psychotherapy*, XIX, p. 302–308, 1965

Voigt, Ch., Kleinklassenarbeit in der Volksschule, in: Kirchhoff, H., Pietrowicz, B., Kontaktgestörte Kinder, *Psychol. Praxis*, 29, Basel, 1961

Vuckovich, D.M., Pediatric neurology and learning disabilities, in: Myklebust, H.R. (ed.): *Progress in learning disabilities*, Vol. I, New York, p. 16–38, 1968

Wender, P.H., *Minimal brain dysfunction in children*, New York, 1971

Werner, R., *Das verhaltensgestörte Kind. Heilpädagogik psychischer Fehlhaltungen*, Berlin (East), 1967

White, R.; Lippitt, R.V., Leader behavior and member reaction in three 'social climates', in: Cartwright, D.; Zander, A. (eds.): *Group dynamics. Research and theory*, New York, 1960[2]

Wilson, G.; Ryland, G., *Social group work practice. The creative use of the social process*, Boston, 1949

Witkin, H.A. et al., *Psychological differentiation. Studies of development*, New York, 1962

Yalom, I.D., *The theory and practice of group psychotherapy*, New York, 1970

Zander, A., Resistance to change. Its analysis and prevention, in: Bennis, W.G.; Benne, K.D.; Chin, R. (eds.): *The planning of change. Readings in the applied behavioral sciences*, New York, p. 543–548, 1961

Zander, A., *Motives and goals in groups*, New York, 1971

Zulliger, H., *Heilende Kräfte im kindlichen Spiel*, Bern, 1952

Zulliger, H., *Schwierige Kinder*, Bern, 1953

Zulliger, H., *Bausteine zur Kinderpsychotherapie*, Bern, 1957

Structopathic children

Contents Part II. Results of experimental research of structuring group therapy